New Views

on

Luke and Acts

New Views

on

Luke and Acts

Edited by

Earl Richard

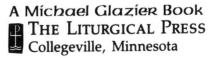

A Michael Glazier Book
THE LITURGICAL PRESS
Collegeville, Minnesota

A Michael Glazier Book
published by
THE LITURGICAL PRESS

Cover design by David Manahan, O.S.B.
The Annunciation is from an ivory panel (chair of Maximianus) in Ravenna, Italy.

Typography by Phyllis Boyd LeVane

1   2   3   4   5   6   7   8   9

Library of Congress Cataloging-in-Publication Data

New views on Luke and Acts / edited by Earl Richard.
        p.   cm.
    "A Michael Glazier book."
    Includes bibliographical references and index.
    ISBN 0-8146-5704-4 (pbk.)
    1. Bible.   N.T.   Luke—Criticism, interpretation, etc.   2. Bible.
    N.T.   Acts—Criticism, interpretation, etc.   I. Richard, Earl.
BS2589.N48   1990
226.4'06—dc20   90-62044
                                                                   CIP

Contents

Preface

With the advent of redaction criticism following World War II, Luke, along with other Synoptic writers, received considerable attention, for the Third Gospel and the Acts of the Apostles were increasingly appreciated as literary creations rather than the juxtaposition of preformed oral units or written sources, as scholars had earlier maintained. It was particularly the work of Hans Conzelmann for the gospel[1] and that of Ernst Haenchen for the Acts of the Apostles[2] (both in the mid-50s) which established the creative role of Luke as theologian and writer. Building upon the insights of H.J. Cadbury[3] and Martin Dibelius,[4] scholars lent their efforts to understanding Luke's use of the Jesus tradition in composing a narrative about the master and of early community lore in putting together the first account of Christian beginnings.

After two decades of relatively negative assessment, especially during the 60s and early 70s,[5] evaluation of Luke's work took a decidedly positive and creative direction. With the appearance of new monographs and commentaries on Luke-Acts and an increasing number of scholarly seminars and dissertations devoted to Lukan concerns, this author has once again emerged as the focus of historical, literary, and theological interest.[6] Part of this renewed dialogue has been the Luke-Acts Task Force of the Catholic Biblical Association which, beginning in 1976, met under the direction of Robert F. O'Toole, S.J. The present volume is by and large the product of the final years of that biblical seminar.

The substance of the volume consists of eight essays written by members of the task force and reviewed by seminar colleagues. These contributions represent a range of methodological and thematic concerns and offer the reader a sampling both of the scope and level of current Lukan scholarship. The

* Notes for the Preface can be found on p. 163

7

collection of exegetical studies (part two) opens with Judette Kolasny's interesting form and rhetorical study of Luke's paradigmatic Nazareth episode and is followed by Thomas Brodie's intriguing claim that the genre of Luke-Acts must be understood in light of the Septuagint version of the Elijah-Elisha cycle. For his part, Marion Soards tackles the debated issue of the source of Luke's passion narrative by offering a convincing analysis of the mockery scene and its narrative function. Lastly, Eloise Rosenblatt creatively applies G. Genette's narrative analysis to Paul's Jerusalem speech. These studies illustrate well the wide range of methodological approaches which Lukan scholars routinely apply to the examination of that author's work.

The third group of essays consists of four studies of varying methodologies and theological interests. The first is a survey of the theme of discipleship, wherein Dennis Sweetland examines Luke's concept of following Jesus on the way. Employing a lexical approach Robert Mowery notes the Lukan references to God the Father and analyzes their function in the overall narrative. By means of lexical and narrative criticism, Earl Richard examines the coming/granting of the Spirit as a recurring theme first in the life of Jesus and then, extensively, in that of the community. Richard Cassidy addresses Luke's political stance by focusing on Paul's non-Roman opponents in the narrative of Acts. Repeatedly, from these essays the reader is able to discern the status of Lukan scholarship on various issues and to glean new insights and challenges for further thought and research.

The first section of the volume has a slightly different origin from the other essays. All three studies were commissioned with this particular work and readership in mind. All three attempt to situate Luke in different but interrelated contexts: Luke, the Christian writer who focuses on the Christian community and its concerns (Dennis Sweetland); Luke, the Greco-Roman writer who is heir to the Jewish tradition of the early community and is a citizen of the Greco-Roman world (Marion Soards); and, lastly, Luke, the author who has a distinct style, strategy, and message (Earl Richard). The three essays address general issues and prepare for the more specialized studies of the remainder of the volume.

The intended readership of this collection of articles, therefore, is threefold. The introductory essays address the relative beginner in biblical studies as well as those who do not specialize in Luke-Acts. These are provided with an overview of Luke, the early Christian writer. The principal reader of this collection, however, is the biblical student and teacher who requires a relatively comprehensive survey of Lukan studies in terms of content and methodology. Both teacher and student will find in these essays an excellent companion to the actual text of Luke and Acts. At the same time, the editors are convinced that a number of these essays break new ground and offer a challenge to other NT scholars. Luke has much to offer; this volume, it is hoped, will provide information, incentive, and insight to the reader of the Third Gospel and the Acts of the Apostles.

Special thanks are owed Robert O'Toole as director of the Luke-Acts Task Force, Dennis Sweetland and Marion Soards as generous and insightful assistant editors, and Loyola University for providing editorial funding.

Abbreviations

AusBR	*Australian Biblical Review*
BAGD	*Greek-English Lexicon of the NT* (eds. Bauer et al)
Bib	*Biblica*
BibLeb	*Bibel und Leben*
BR	*Biblical Research*
BTB	*Biblical Theology Bulletin*
BZ	*Biblische Zeitschrift*
CBQ	*Catholic Biblical Quarterly*
EstBib	*Estudios biblicos*
ETL	*Ephemerides theologicae lovanienses*
EvT	*Evangelische Theologie*
ExpTim	*Expository Times*
IB	*Interpreter's Bible*
IDB	*Interpreter's Dictionary of the Bible*
IDBSup	Supplementary volume to *IDB*
Int	*Interpretation*
JBC	*Jerome Biblical Commentary*
JBL	*Journal of Biblical Literature*
JJS	*Journal of Jewish Studies*
JQR	*Jewish Quarterly Review*
JRS	*Journal of Roman Studies*
JSNT	*Journal for the Study of the New Testament*
LTK	*Lexikon für Theologie und Kirche*
Neot	*Neotestamentica*
NovT	*Novum Testamentum*
NTS	*New Testament Studies*
Numen	*Numen: International Review for the History of Religions*
OCD	*Oxford Classical Dictionary*
PCB	*Peake's Commentary on the Bible*

PRS	*Perspectives in Religious Studies*
RAC	*Reallexikon für Antike und Christentum*
RB	*Revue biblique*
RevRel	*Review for Religious*
RHPR	*Revue d'histoire et de philosophie religieuses*
RTP	*Revue de théologie et de philosophie*
RTR	*Reformed Theological Review*
SB	*Scripture Bulletin*
SBL	Society of Biblical Literature
SBT	*Studia biblica et theologica*
ScEccl	*Sciences ecclésiastiques*
ScEs	*Science et esprit*
SJT	*Scottish Journal of Theology*
ST	*Studia theologica*
TBT	*The Bible Today*
TDNT	*Theological Dictionary of the New Testament*
TLZ	*Theologische Literaturzeitung*
TR	*Theology Review*
TRu	*Theologische Rundschau*
TS	*Theological Studies*
VSpir	*Vie spirituelle*
ZKT	*Zeitschrift für katholische Theologie*
ZNW	*Zeitschrift für die neutestamentliche Wissenschaft*

PART I

*General Introduction
to the
Work of Luke*

1

Luke: Author and Thinker

Earl Richard

The plan of this essay is inspired by an observation of Lucian of Samosata, a near-contemporary of Luke (*fl.* 165 A.D.), who maintained that a good historian possesses two fundamental qualities: "political understanding and power of expression," i.e., a masterful ability to comprehend events and the requisite skill to communicate these effectively. He claims that the former is "a gift of nature" while the latter is the result of "much work, discipline, and imitation of the ancients."[1] Thus, these two qualities, labelled thought and art or theology and style, along with Luke's literary product, will provide the focus of the three parts of the essay: writer, literary work, thinker. So we turn our attention to one of the NT's premier Hellenistic writers, Luke, the evangelist and historian.

1. Luke the Author

Whether in terms of grammar, vocabulary, and style, of rhetorical strategy, use of literary conventions, or communicative skill, Luke is given a high rating. Among NT writers, this author ranks among those who have the best command of the Greek language and is one of its most versatile and literarily accomplished.

LUKE THE HELLENISTIC WRITER

When one picks up Luke-Acts, one discerns a more elegant style than that of the other evangelists, greater consciousness of time and space factors, and a broader perspective on the Christ-event and its consequent Jesus movement. Further,

Luke's work takes in both the Jewish and the Hellenistic components of the early tradition and weds these into an interesting perspective on the new movement.

In Acts and sometimes in the gospel one encounters a moderately classical command of Greek, a style which has its finest expression in the periodic sentence of the prologue (Luke 1:1-4). Following this, however, one is confronted by a different style, a Semitic form of Greek replete with parallelisms, Semitic idioms, and a marked absence of the refinements of Hellenistic style. This type of writing is found particularly in the infancy narratives (Luke 1-2) which are an attempt to imitate the style and tone of the Septuagint, the Semitized Greek version of the scriptures. Further, this section receives an added Semitizing element from Luke's relentless use of a paratactic style, that is, the repeated juxtaposition of short, related clauses either without or with simple connecting words or phrases.

Subsequently there is a lessening of this style, and a greater variety and complexity of sentence structure and vocabulary emerge. Luke, for example, favors the optative mood, genitive absolute, and other stylistic niceties, employs a sophisticated vocabulary for emphasis and variety,[2] and is usually faithful to the idomatic tendencies of Greek style (e.g., the proper use of participles).[3] In contrast, one should note the anomalous use, often in juxtaposition, of the standard singular of "sky" (*ouranos*) with the plural (Luke 10:20, 21; Acts 7:55, 56) or the genitive with the verb "to hear" (*akouō*) with the less-than-correct accusative (Luke 16:29, 31; Acts 9:4, 7). Such phenomena are an indication both of stylistic ability and respect for the tradition used[4] and make the use or translation of Semitic sources by Luke doubtful.[5]

In accordance with contemporary literary custom, the author employs interlocking prologues for Luke and Acts, prologues which reveal a literarily and historically conscious writer. Luke knows that others have preceded as ministers of the word and narrators of the events of Jesus' life. Thus, the narrative will be the result of accurate research and interpretation and so will be trustworthy (1:1-4).[6] When told with hyperbole that the movement did not emerge in a hidden corner (Acts 26:26), the reader senses that Luke's composition is a historically conscious activity. Indeed, providing synchronisms for the story's time setting, the author relates the events of Jesus' life to the reigns of emperors, kings, governors, and Jewish authorities (Luke 1-3). Christianity has taken its place on the stage of history, for it is a universal movement whose founder, through narrative anticipation, initiated the Jewish and Gentile missions (sending of the twelve and the seventy, Luke 9:1f; 10:1f), a theme which is prominent in Simeon's words (Luke 2:32), in the message of the banquet (14:15f), and in the discussion at the Jerusalem council (Acts 15).[7] It also forms an inclusio for the two works, since the unusual expression "the salvation of God" near the beginning of Luke (3:6) and at the end of Acts (28:28) stresses the universalist motif in the author's thought.[8]

Possibly pointing to the author's Greek background is the presentation of the Christ-event and the spread of the movement in a favorable way to Hellenistic contemporaries. Jesus and his followers are declared innocent (Luke 23; Acts 26);[9] Roman and other officials are sympathetically presented (centurions, Pilate, Cornelius, Gallio, Agrippa). Nonetheless, the theme of innocence is subordinate to that of righteousness and so motivated more by religious than by political concerns,[10] for Luke's treatment of Jewish and Roman authorities owes less to historical reminiscences or apologetics than to a perception of social, political structures and concern for continuity.

Luke's Gospel is similar to Hellenistic biography.[11] The author has borrowed genre and content from Mark and has extended the time-line in both directions. Jesus' story is expanded to include resurrection appearances and his departure and, on into Acts, his intercession vis-à-vis his followers. Luke has extended the time-line forward to include annunciation and birth stories to underscore the growth of the story's hero (Luke 2:40, 52). Thus, the virginal conception of Jesus indicates not a higher christology, as in Matthew, but rather meets the requirements of biography wherein heroes are attributed divine origins, unusual births, or prophetical omens.[12]

Luke has modified the story itself to make it a pliable instrument for a new perspective. Scenes are recast and materials added to emphasize the journey to Jerusalem (Luke 9:51f) or Jesus' challenge to Jew and Gentile (5:17f). In the latter Luke has recast Markan controversies and rewritten the introduction to present Jesus to a jury of his contemporaries, who are unable to convict him of wrongdoing (6:11). In other instances Luke, following classical and biblical conventions and employing traditional sayings, structures the last-supper episode into a farewell address or testamentary banquet for Jesus' last instructions (22:14-38) or has made "redactional use of the Hellenistic symposium ... to organize ... traditional material" (Luke 7:36-50; 11:37-54; 14:1-24).[13]

Luke modifies episodes and adds new ones to balance stories about men and women, John and Jesus, word and deed.[14] Such modifications are done from a universalist perspective, which contrasts high and low (1:51-52; 14:7-11), proud and humble (18:9-14), rich and poor (4:18; 6:20, 24; 16:19-31). The good news is addressed to the dispossessed ("the poor, maimed, lame, blind," 14:13, 21), for salvation is for "all flesh" (3:6). Also, Luke's story stretches from Adam in temporal terms to "the end of the earth" in geographical terms (Luke 3:38; Acts 1:8).[15]

The second volume makes more effective use of dramatic and rhetorical techniques, the qualities of ancient history writing. Further, it is replete with stock scenes, but contrary to its closest analogue, the historical monograph,[16] it offers not political and military scenes, but trials, jail episodes, missionary encounters, a farewell speech, and a sea voyage with a requisite shipwreck scene.[17] Luke makes abundant use of speeches, about one third of Acts. There are character-sketches, prefaces, appeal to omens or visions, and conscious use of parallelism. The student of Greco-Roman literature is familiar with the period's love for symmetry and parallels and with the historian's generous use of literary conventions. Thus, Luke's practice in doing research and in composing narratives matches the theory of the period.[18] Luke is a Hellenistic writer for whom fact and story along with literary conventions are at the service of the writer's view of things. The latter were tools of the narrator to convey a message to the story's intended readers. It is in this sense that Luke is a literary historian and theologian.

Luke was less free in composing the gospel, since the material and genre had received their shape from Mark and since these had become part of the tradition. Still, the author felt free to restructure the story and to employ current literary conventions to compose a new life of Jesus. The narrative introduces speeches, effectively uses dramatic techniques, and constructs parallels and thematic sequences as its hero is led to Jerusalem for the story's climax. Thus, in Luke-Acts, one encounters a Hellenist Christian who addresses the reader, aware of the movement's debt to Israel and of its Roman socio-political and religious milieu.

COMPOSITION OF THE GOSPEL AND ACTS

For the first of these works, the author's dependence on Mark is hardly to be doubted. The gospel regularly follows Mark for the order of episodes, so much so that most departures from this sequence are explained in terms of Lukan redaction.[19] Additionally, much of the content of Jesus' life is also borrowed from that source. Luke usually modifies Mark's weak grammar and style but remains faithful to its content and vocabulary. Thus, Luke borrows from Mark the essential elements of episodes but tends to alter these in style and detail (see Luke's treatment of the baptism scene, 3:21-22). Such rewriting produces a more complex and elegant style and provides clues to numerous Lukan concerns.

Beyond the addition of a prologue and birth stories (chaps 1-2) and resurrection appearances in Jerusalem (chap 24), the basic outline of Jesus' life follows that of Mark, for, apart from the occasional transposition of episodes, Luke imposes on it only three major modifications: one omission (elimination of Mark 6:45-8:26 at 9:17—note also the minor omission of Mark 9:42-10:12 at 9:50) and two interpolations (additions of 6:20-8:3 and 9:51-18:14 to the Markan sequence). These changes are variously motivated; in some instances Luke expands the Markan narrative by supplementing it with data from Q (Matthew and Luke's non-Markan source) or from oral tradition; in others the writer adds blocks of new narrative and discourse material.

After a stylized prologue, one encounters an extended two-part narrative about John the Baptist and Jesus. The first, spanning the first two chapters (1:5-2:52) and consisting of two annunciation stories (one dealing with John's father and the other with Jesus' mother), the meeting of the two mothers, dual birth narratives, and the temple scene, derives from Luke's own traditions. The second section, which pursues the contrast between John and Jesus (3:1-4:13), follows for the most part the Markan schema to which Q and L materials (Luke's oral tradition) have been added to underscore the role and teaching of John, Jesus' genealogy, and his temptations. In the case of the last mentioned, Luke finds a simple statement that Jesus was "tempted by Satan" (Mark 1:12-13) and supplements this by a threefold encounter of Jesus with his eschatological rival.

If the section on the Galilean ministry (4:14-9:50) follows Mark, there are traces of Lukan reorganization, the most blatant of which is the moving forward of the Nazareth episode, which Luke expands into a programmatic statement of Jesus' ministry (4:16-30). Also, within this section there occurs a major Lukan addition, 6:20-8:3, consisting of the sermon on the plain, miracles, and a delegation from John the Baptist. The last mentioned relates to the Nazareth episode and the program mapped out for God's envoy. Lastly, through the rewriting of Markan episodes, Luke structures chapter 9 around a series of responses to Herod's question: "who is this about whom I hear such things?" (9:9). Thus, the chapter functions as a christological inquiry.[20]

The journey to Jerusalem (9:51-21:38), as a construct, is a Lukan creation. Taking a cue from Mark 10:1, which notes that Jesus left Galilee and made his way to Judaea, Luke brings together Q and L material and organizes this into a journey from Galilee to the Judaean capital. The section opens up with Jesus resolutely heading toward the city of fulfilment, conscious of his destiny (9:51). During this long journey Jesus discourses on numerous themes (discipleship, love of God and neighbor, prayer, eschatological warning, mercy, forgiveness, perseverance) and confronts the Jewish authorities. Repeatedly during the journey the reader hears that Jesus is making his way to the holy city: 13:22, 33; 17:11; 18:31 (already at 9:31).

The Jerusalem ministry (19:28-21:38) follows the Markan outline faithfully although the author indulges in minor editorial work, such as the addition of sayings concerning the city and its fate and about the end-times.

The final section, 22:1-24:53, is also dependent on Mark for the basic sequence and the majority of episodes, for Luke omits episodes or details, adds or expands others, displaces some elements of the sequence, and attends to small touches which underscore a new perspective. The anointing at Bethany is omitted because Luke has a parallel tradition (the woman with the ointment, 7:36-50), which is placed at an earlier point to emphasize forgiveness. Luke also tends to simplify multiple traditions by elimination; only one multiplication story and one mockery scene are retained. Elements of Jesus' trial are either eliminated, because Luke insists on a religious cause for Jesus' death, or transferred to the trials of Stephen or Paul. Twice Luke eliminates or modifies the promise of Galilean appearances (22:39; 24:6) because of the role assigned to Jerusalem, where all resurrection appearances occur. Also, Lukan modifications lessen the accountability of Pilate (Jesus is three times declared innocent, 23:4f) and underscore the responsibility of the Jewish authorities (23:23, 25).[21] The resurrection stories, apart from the empty tomb episode, have no Markan parallels and so derive from special Lukan material; these include the Emmaus story, the appearance in Jerusalem, the final commission, and Jesus' ascension.

From the beginning Luke announces the scope of Acts (1:8): a threefold mission to Jerusalem (2:1-8:4), to Palestine and beyond (8:5-12:25), and to the end of the earth (13:1-28:31).[22] The narrative allows its characters to express their witness to the risen Lord throughout the Roman provinces of the East, Greece, and Rome itself. After some preliminaries (a prologue, narrative overlap with the ending of the gospel, and an account of the reconstitution of the twelve), Luke records at length and in physical terms the coming of the Father's promise. For six chapters the beginnings in Jerusalem of the growing mission, the community and its life, and the ever-worsening series of trials (warnings, beatings, and death of a Christian witness) are chronicled. As a result of Stephen's death or, in Lukan terms, owing to God's hidden purpose (5:38-39), the mission spreads through Palestine: Samaria, Judaea, and further north into Antioch. The role of Peter is central until the arrival of Luke's hero, Saul of Tarsus, who becomes the principal character for the remainder of the story.

Through successive and ever-expanding journeys, interrupted by a meeting of leaders in Jerusalem, and after several indecisive trials, Paul, in spite of a dramatic shipwreck off the coast of Malta, arrives in Rome. There Luke, with Paul as spokesman, comments on the situation of the mission; Israel is divided in its assessment of the Jesus movement, but the Gentile world offers promise for missionary activity (28:24, 28).[23] Thus, Luke the optimist, brings the curtain down on an open-ended mission with Paul welcoming all and preaching "openly and unhindered" about God's kingdom and the Lord Jesus Christ.

What sources did Luke employ to compose Acts? Earlier studies that had postulated Jerusalemite and Antiochene traditions or Hellenistic and Hebrew sources are not supported by recent redaction and composition analysis.[24] Today, it is popularly affirmed 1) that Luke was a companion of Paul (Phlm 24; Col 4:14: "our beloved physician") and 2) that this was indicated by the use of "we" in the later chapters of Acts (16, 20-21, 27-28). Also, others insist 3) that the writer employed an eyewitness' diary for the last third of the narrative. This last proposal fails to convince since there is no perceptible difference in style between the "we sections" and the rest of Acts. As to the first two there are insurmountable objections to their plausibility. The name Luke is traditional, dating back to the time of Marcion in the second century. That a person by that name was a fellow worker of Paul is clear from Philemon 24; but that such a person would have been a traveler with Paul, the author of Acts, and, therefore, the one responsible for the Pauline speeches of Acts, is hard to believe. The author has no firsthand knowledge of Pauline thought nor of Paul's letters. The solution which best explains the anomalies is that its author is an anonymous post-apostolic Christian, who, like the Paulinist authors, was acquainted with the stories circulating about the apostle to the Gentiles.[25] The "we-sections," I believe, owe to a literary convention sometimes employed in sea voyages and not an eyewitness account.[26] The sources of Acts are unknown to us but we can surmise the use of a growing community lore about the "old days," by an author who did personal research while traveling and who questioned the remaining "eyewitnesses and ministers of the word."

2. Developmental Character of Luke's Work

Scholarship insists that Luke and Acts not be studied in isolation, for they are related in style, thematic perspective, and planning. The two begin with elegant prologues, addressed to Theophilus, an unknown person of high standing. The second refers back to the earlier work and presents a short resume of the gospel: "in the earlier book, Theophilus, I dealt with all Jesus began to do and teach, until the day he was taken up" (Acts 1:1-2).

LUKE-ACTS AS A TWO-VOLUME WORK

Numerous parallels exist between these works. Leaving aside the birth narratives, one notes their strikingly similar beginnings: dominant role of the Spirit and key initial speeches enshrined within parallel programmatic narratives (Luke 3-4; Acts 2). The part played by John the Baptist at the beginning of the gospel (3:1f) has its balanced references in Acts 1 (vv. 5, 22). As the Spirit comes down on Jesus at the baptism scene, leads him into the wilderness to be tempted, empowers him, and dwells in him for the ministry, so that same, promised Spirit comes down on the assembled community at Pentecost, accompanied by signs of the end-days (Acts 2). As the Spirit acted in Jesus' ministry so it acts in that of his followers (2:38).

To set the stage for Jesus' ministry Luke borrows from Mark (6:1-6) a narrative about Jesus' rejection by his townspeople, an episode which is restructured to express "in a nutshell" the good news which Jesus preaches and is.[27] By means of an OT citation, Luke lays out the messianic program which Jesus' life is to personify in his concern for the "poor, mained, blind, and lame" (4:18-19). Further, the author appeals to the Elijah and Elisha stories of 1-2 Kings to comment on Judaeo-Christian relations. The Nazareth episode with its speech and rejection encapsulates the promise and foreboding of the life of God's Messiah.

The parallel episode which launches Acts is the pentecost narrative with its kerygmatic speech. Among its central themes are the universal mission, the eschatological nature of the Christian experience, salvation in the Name, and the risen

Lord who pours out the promised Spirit. The key to both works is "Jesus of Nazareth, a man attested ... by God," who was delivered up, crucified, and raised "according to the definite plan and foreknowledge of God" (Acts 2:22-24), the one in whose name there is salvation (4:12).

Another structural parallel involves Luke 24:36-53 and Acts 1:3-13. The first volume concludes with Jesus speaking about the mission which is to begin in Jerusalem, where the disciples, after receiving the Spirit, will become Jesus' witnesses. The disciples then observe him ascend into heaven and return to Jerusalem where they worship in the temple. To assist the reader of the second work Luke restates, with some variation, the themes of the concluding verses of the gospel. The theme of John's water baptism is added as a contrast to baptism with the Holy Spirit (Acts 1:5) and Luke now indicates not only the mission's point of departure but also its point of arrival (Acts 1:8).

The gospel ends with the disciples "in the temple" but in Acts 1:13 they are in "the upper room." This shift in locale is significant and signals Luke's decision to continue the story. Luke is interested in narrating not only the promise with which the gospel ends but also the actualization of that promise in the life of the community. Thus, the disciples are afforded a unique association with the risen Lord before his ascension, for he appears, speaks of the kingdom, eats with them, and trains them for forty days (a parallel to Jesus' own forty days and an allusion to the ideal time of preparation for disciples). The choice of the upper room as the locale for launching the mission is an important christological and ecclesiological statement.

Interesting parallels are drawn between Jesus and his followers; as the master raises men and women from the dead (Luke 7:11-17; 8:40-56) so do his disciples, Peter and Paul (Acts 9:36-43; 20:7-12); as Jesus has an introductory speech so do Peter and Paul (Luke 4; Acts 4; 13). Paralleling Jesus' farewell discourse is that of Paul at Miletus (Luke 21; Acts 20). Episodes in Acts are composed with an eye to parallels in the gospel; the trials of Jesus relate to those of Stephen and Paul; Luke 9:5 and 10:11 promise what is accomplished in Acts 13:51 and 18:6; Acts 28:7-8 about Paul and Publius' father is parallel to Luke 4:38-39 about Jesus and Peter's mother-in-law.

ACTS AS A CONTINUATION OF THE GOSPEL

The two works are also related in subject matter, for the first tells Jesus' life and the second dwells on the activity of the "absent" Lord.[28] Jesus is center stage in the gospel, while in Acts he is not far off in the wings. He acts through intermediaries and directly in the vision of Stephen or in the call and instruction of Paul (Acts 7; 9). Acts is also centered on the Christ-event, but because of a change in time period (post-resurrection era) and genre (monograph about Jesus' followers and the divinely sanctioned mission), the master's role is reduced only in appearance. Acts is the logical sequel to the gospel.[29]

If Acts continues Luke's original project, how then is one to describe the temporal scheme of Luke-Acts? This is relevant in view of claims that Luke betrayed the kerygma in deciding to compose Acts, that is, in being more interested in history, organization, and doctrine than in Jesus and faith in him. The author was invariably judged on the basis of H. Conzelmann's threefold schema for Luke-Acts: the time of Israel, the time of Jesus (the middle or perfect time—but in the past nonetheless), and the time of the church. Wisely, scholarship now rejects this schema and proposes a standard twofold temporal outline: the Old Age (the time of Israel as preparation, prophecy, and promise) and the New Age (inaugurated by the Christ-event and awaiting the final consummation). Luke, having inherited the apocalyptic schema of contemporary Judaism and the early Jesus movement, situates within it and reinterprets in light of that schema the Christ-event for a new generation.[30] This is not where Luke's originality lies and not where one might accuse the author of betrayal. Instead, the Lukan community and its evangelist were concerned about continuity between Israel and Christianity and about the relationship between the period of Jesus' life and that of the community. The gospel is the story of the master's life among his disciples and Acts shows how the now-departed Jesus is Lord of the community and present to its members.

The period of promise does not constitute a part of Luke-Acts in a structural sense since the gospel begins with Jesus' life. Instead the Old Age permeates the work of Luke who strives to show how that part of God's plan prepared for "the last days" (Acts 2:17). Terminology of promise, prophecy, and actualization (e.g., Luke 3:4; 7:27; Acts 4:25; 7:40; 15:15) underscores the continuity in God's design for humanity between the time of Israel and the new and final epoch of salvation. So Luke ends the gospel with a twofold insistence that Jesus' life, passion, and resurrection are part of God's plan as foretold in scripture and had to be fulfilled (24:26-27, 44-46), an argument which becomes a motif of the kerygmatic speeches of Acts.

If the time of Israel is in the background, that of Jesus is at the center of Luke-Acts. Luke's presentation of the Christ-event, from birth through death to return, is offered in stages: first, the time of Jesus' ministry when he performs mighty works and reveals the Father; second, the central section which is devoted to the kerygma, namely, Jesus' passion, death, and resurrection; and third, the time when the absent Jesus operates within the community. The gospel narrative opens with an OT-like introduction to Jesus' public ministry; the figures of Zechariah, Simeon, and Anna, also John the Baptist, are given prophetic qualities. Jesus' ministry is a perfect time when Satan's activity is reduced to a minimum (4:13; 22:3) and "glorious things" (13:17) are done by Jesus that all might "glorify God" (5:26). He is presented as the righteous servant who does God's deeds before a jury of experts which is unable to convict him (5:17; 6:11; 14:6; 20:26; 40). It is the time of ministry to poor, outcast, to all, "the acceptable year of the Lord," the year of reprieve (4:19; 13:6-9).

The central period (Luke 22 through Acts 2) is devoted to the nucleus of the Christian message, the death and resurrection (threated below in relation to christology). This segment then consists of the passion and death, the resurrection, the departure of Jesus, and the resolution of his absence in the pentecostal narrative.

To present the final stage, Luke employs three ecclesial models: 1) that of the idealized Jerusalem community, 2) that centered around Antioch and its missionary activity, and 3) that reflected in the Miletus speech, a farewell address which terminates Paul's missionary journeys and looks forward to Luke's time.[31] These models are skillfully interconnected as one period leads into another, as themes are pursued from episode to episode, and as the community increases and multiplies. An effective technique employed to interrelate the stages of Luke and Acts is the narrative appropriation of the dictum: like master like disciples. As Jesus prayed, preached, suffered, so the disciples are portrayed as doing the same.

Luke and Acts are companion volumes whose interrelationship results from similarity of content and style and from conscious literary and theological creation; Acts is more than an "afterthought."[32] Indeed, I maintain that the third evangelist, whose original text would have been closer in structure to Mark, at a later date, convinced that a companion volume was needed, composed a sequel (with revision of the former) as a continuation of the gospel.[33]

3. Luke the Thinker

Luke's vision of the Christian reality has a definite historical setting: origin and matrix in Judaism and its scriptures, embedded in the story of Jesus and his followers, and at work throughout the Roman empire;[34] it has a philosophical-theological framework: "the definite plan and foreknowledge of God" (Acts 2:23); and offers an unrelenting christological forcus: a finely articulated agency christology. It is to these themes that we now turn.

LUKAN PORTRAIT OF JESUS

Jesus, for Luke, is first and foremost a man who has won God's approval; he does mighty works as God's Messiah (Luke 9:20; Acts 2:22). He is the envoy which the Jewish scriptures promised, yet is destined to be the vehicle of universal salvation. At the outset Jesus is placed within a Palestinian cultural ambiance, for Luke underscores his Jewish background: genealogy, synchronisms, familiarity with the scriptures, Nazarene upbringing, and customary association with the synagogue. Also, the author retains from Mark the blind man's address of Jesus as "Son of David" and adds two stories where first a woman and then a man are approvingly referred to as children of Abraham (13:16; 19:9). Nonetheless, he is situated upon a Hellenistic stage. He can trace his roots to noteworthy Jewish ancestors and to the father of the human race (3:38). He has come to seek the lost sheep of Israel and to bring salvation to "all flesh" (3:6). We should recall Luke's universal character and the gospel's many intimations of the Gentile mission.

Luke's Jesus is the most humanly appealing of the gospel portraits. Jesus' fondness for poor and outcast is well known, for a favorite Lukan theme is Jesus' care for "the poor, mained, lame, blind." Also, he is accused of "receiving sinners and eating with them," of paying special attention to sinners, to outcast lepers and Samaritans, and to other disadvantaged people. In regard to the last, one should note the expanded role of women in Jesus' ministry and in Luke-Acts generally. Jesus is made to say: "blessed are you poor" and also "woe to you that are rich" (6:20, 24). It is principally Luke who attributes to Jesus such traits as forgiveness, mercy, love of enemy, stress on giving, joy, and frequent prayer. Luke also adds humanistic touches to traditional stories; children are given back to their parents (7:15; 9:42); Jesus commands that a little girl be provided with food (8:55); and a guard receives Jesus' healing touch (22:51).

An array of christological titles is used, both the traditional: "Son of God," "Son of Man," "Lord," "Christ" and the unusual: "Servant" and "Savior." Occasionally Luke adds the title "Son of God" to Markan narratives, twice in the temptation story and once at the end of a summary, but on the whole Luke follows Mark. The title "Son of God" is extended to Jesus' childhood and employed twice in Acts. "Son of Man," though more frequent, is applied by Luke in a way consistent with Markan usage; it is applied to Jesus' ministry, death and resurrection, and eschatological role. "Lord" (*kyrios*) is a favorite of Luke's Gospel, where the "distinction between the earthly and the exalted Lord" has become blurred and Jesus' lordship is claimed for the entire Christ-event.[35] Other titles, "including Servant of God, the Holy One, the Righteous One

... Author of life (Leader), Savior and Son of God," have become "different ways of calling Jesus 'the Christ.'"[36] This is also the usage one finds in the kerygmatic speeches of Acts.

Titles then play a different role in Luke than they do in Mark. In the former they are often used interchangeably while in the latter they usually retain their specific meanings. If in Mark the title "Christ" sometimes serves as a bridge between christological appellations, in Luke this occurs on a larger scale. Even the title "Savior" (used only four times in Luke's work) is thus used. From this we conclude that it is not the original meaning of the titles that is important but their use in Luke's overall schema. For example, while the title "Savior" is infrequent and lacks specificity, the related concept of "salvation" is a major theme from the beginning of Luke to the end of Acts.

If there is a central christological title for Luke, it is "Christ" which claims that distinction since it serves as a bridge (as it had in Mark) for Luke's descriptions of Jesus and because of the importance such phrases as "the Christ of God" and "Jesus is the Christ" have for Luke. Indeed, the expression "the Christ of God," which serves as Peter's confession (9:20), provides a major clue to understanding Luke's notion of the divine plan.

THE DIVINE PLAN AND JESUS' ROLE THEREIN

Luke-Acts' perception of the history of salvation is all encompassing, for its author sees God's plan for humanity as foretold by the prophets of old, realized by the divine visitation of God's Son, and actualized through select intermediaries in the last days. The theme of the divine purpose imbues Luke's perception of the Christ-event and the author misses few opportunities to reflect on this overarching theme. Terms and episodes that express divine agency or necessity are employed and various types of supernatural intervention are emphasized. Luke also favors a variety of temporal expressions to stress the divine plan and appeals to the actualization of the scriptures.[37]

Central to this concept is Luke's stress on divine activity; all aspects of the plan of salvation are viewed theologically. It is God who plans, controls, and directs human events. Jesus is the one sent by God as agent, Son, prophet of the Most High, the obedient one, the one who does God's work (Acts 2:22). Salvation history is defined as God's mighty works and Jesus is the one par excellence who accomplishes these acts. OT prophecy and the books of Moses are viewed as speech of God, who spoke through these about the "now" of salvation. The community, its witnesses, even the Spirit who operates freely within the community, are intermediaries, for God is in control. Statistically, for example, the occurrence of the word "God" is much higher than for the other evangelists. Besides, to underscore divine agency and control, Luke often enhances the role of the Spirit, of angels, and other supernatural phenomena.

Luke's favorite word for expressing the theme of divine necessity is *dei* ("it is necessary that"), a term which occurs 41 times in Luke-Acts and 61 times in the remainder of the New Testament. It is borrowed from Mark for the first passion prediction (Luke 9:22) and becomes a favorite Lukan expression. This word comes from ordinary speech and expresses the neutral necessity of the Hellenistic concept of fate. In the hands of biblical writers of an earlier period the term encompassed the concept of the personal will of a living God, who is in control of life, cosmic affairs, and human history and who gives them direction and purpose. Luke too believes God intervenes in human affairs to achieve salvation for humanity and uses *dei* to underscore the wide variety of elements which make up the divine plan.[38]

Luke expanded the use of *dei* in the gospel to speak of Jesus doing God's work (2:49), of his ministry (4:43), of the passion (9:22; 17:25), of Judaism and the Law (11:42), of the Spirit (12:12), of Jerusalem (13:33), and of God's joy in light of human repentance (15:32). In Acts too it is employed to relate persons and themes to the divine plan: fulfilment of scripture (1:16), eschatological aspect of Luke's christology (3:21), soteriology (4:12), and Paul's role in God's plan (9:6, 16; 19:21; 27:24). Other terms are also used for this concept: "necessary," "determined," "plan," "foreknowledge," and "will." Additionally, Luke alludes to God's plan as follows: "it seemed good to the Holy Spirit and to us" (Acts 15:28), "he set his face to go to Jerusalem," or "it cannot be that a prophet should perish away from Jerusalem" (Luke 9:51; 13:33).

Luke sees God as the mover and the divine plan as guide and goal for human action; its dynamism is the unfolding and working out of this plan in the human sphere. Following the formative era of Israel's relationship with God, Luke sees the New Age dawning with the arrival of a special envoy. This unique episode is presented in a cosmic or divine scope, for God is seen as intervening in history or "making a visitation." The verb "to visit" (*episkeptomai*), a rare LXX term referring to the solemn Day of the Lord, is used on four occasions by Luke. It describes John's role in Luke 1:68, Jesus' ministry in 7:16, Jerusalem's destiny in 19:44, and the Gentile mission in Acts 15:14. Crucial is Luke's use of the term for Jesus' actions among the chosen people: "God has visited his people" (7:16). Jesus is God's gracious visitation to lay claim to what was lost. The concept of visitation of and care for humanity through Jesus then provides unity to Luke's vision of continuity.

So God makes use of intermediaries and Jesus is that agent par excellence, the one who performs God's mighty works. Thus, Luke's work finds its unity and dynamism in its presentation of the person and activity of Jesus Christ as the keystone of the divine plan for salvation. The author has recounted the life of a marvelous individual, Jesus of Nazareth, who is both God's gracious visitation and prophet (Luke 7:16; see also 9:8, 19; 24:19). The latter takes on added importance for Luke who considers Jesus as a prophet who stands in the succession of messengers of God, the prophet like Moses.[39] He is the fulfilment of OT promises, greater than all the prophets, one who does God's will and reveals the Father through preaching and power.

A key to Luke's portrait of Jesus is found in the confession scene, where Peter responds to Jesus' question: "who do you say that I am?" In contrast to the Markan version of the response, "you are the Christ," that of Luke reads: "you are the Christ of God." This qualification is significant and not surprising since in the infancy narratives Luke has the Holy Spirit promise Simeon that he will "not see death before he had seen the Lord's Christ" (2:26). Other passages make the same claim (23:35; Acts 3:13, 18; 4:26, among others), namely, that Jesus' role is that of being God's promised agent. In fact repeatedly in Acts (5:42; 9:22; 17:3; 18:5, 28, especially in the kerygmatic speeches) the object of preaching and confession is the realization that "Jesus was the Christ" (Acts 9:22).

His entire life, from birth to ascension, is the fulfilment of the divine purpose, for his life is conditioned by the journey to Jerusalem (9:51; 13:33; 17:11; 18:31), where, after his death or "exodus" (9:31), he is received (9:51) at God's right hand (Acts 2:33; 7:55-56).[40] His life and death are soteriologically conditioned, i.e., he has come to save what was lost (Luke 15; 19:10). The Christ-event is framed by the concept of "God's salvation" (from Luke 3:6 to Acts 28:28). Indeed, Jesus' whole life is considered redemptive by Luke, for this divine agent has made possible universal salvation in the community of believers through the power of the Spirit.[41]

The two ascension accounts are pivotal in a structural and thematic sense. By means of the first (Luke 24:50-53), Luke brings Jesus' life to a close in the context of the resurrection encounters where the risen Jesus strengthens his followers' faith and establishes them as witnesses and ministers of the world mission.[42] By means of the second and by its association with the pentecost episode (Acts 1-2), Luke grapples more directly with the problem of continuity, for Jesus, established in his heavenly abode, nonetheless continues to be Lord of the community. From his abode with the Father, he acts directly on behalf of his people and, as illustrated in Acts, through his word and the Holy Spirit, who in turn empowers mediators to act in his behalf that all might "seek the Lord" (Acts 15:17).[43]

With the hindsight of Christian faith and the gift of understanding Luke envisioned the Christian experience as the working out of God's purpose with Jesus as agent, i.e., God's prophet and Son bringing salvation (in the gospel) and the risen, "absent" Lord continuing this task through his representatives (in Acts). Thus, God's plan is the center and at the core of this plan is an agent, that perfect human instrument whom God calls my "beloved" or "chosen" Son (Luke 3:22; 9:35). But most of all, for this author Jesus is "the Christ or Messiah of God." It is left then to the reader of Luke-Acts to judge whether Lucian of Samosata would have applauded Luke's literary prowess and intellectual acumen.

2

The Historical and Cultural Setting of Luke-Acts

Marion L. Soards

A commonplace of Luke-Acts studies is the observation that Luke has a keen interest in history. In general, this insight relates to and motivates regular scholarly debate about the historical reliability of information that Luke provides the reader of his two volumes. Luke himself put the modern students of his writings on this line by including several items in his works that are typical of the writings of the historians of his day. Both Luke and Acts begin with formal literary prologues (Luke 1:1-4; Acts 1:1-5) that can be and are compared with the prefaces of such classical and post-classical historical and literary writers as Herodotus, Hippocrates, Josephus, Polybius, and Thucydides.[1] Moreover, Luke repeatedly gives chronological information that declares his intention to set the events he narrates in the context of Greco-Roman and Palestinian history. He relates the birth of Jesus in Bethlehem to a census under Caesar Augustus "when Quirinius was governor of Syria" (Luke 2:1-2);[2] and he dates the appearance of John the Baptist

> in the fifteenth year of the reign of Tiberius Caesar, Pontius Pilate being governor of Judea, and Herod being tetrarch of Galilee, and his brother Philip being tetrarch of the region of Ituraea and Trachonitis, and Lysanias tetrarch of Abilene, in the high-priesthood of Annas and Caiaphas" (Luke 3:1-2).

Strikingly different assessments of Luke's historical accuracy exist among contemporary historians and exegetes.[3] The aim of the present consideration of the historical and cultural setting of Luke-Acts is not, however, to enter the debate about

---

* Notes for Chapter 2 can be found on pp. 165-68

Luke's abilities as a historian; rather this essay seeks to pick up on the lead Luke provides concerning the importance of viewing his work in its own historical and cultural context and attempts to set Luke-Acts in history. Thus the focus here is *Luke-Acts in history* and not *history in Luke-Acts!*[4]

A Starting Point

The world in which Luke lived and the audience to which he wrote was "Hellenized."[5] This state of cultural affairs came about as the result of the military, political, and aesthetic work of Alexander the Great and his successors—Greek, Syrian, Egyptian, and in Luke's time, Roman. The vision for Alexander and the others was to conquer, unify, and rule the world; and the means to the end of unification was "Hellenism."

What were the hallmarks of Hellenistic civilization?[6] To answer this question one must describe the way of life of classical Greece as it was appropriated throughout the regions Alexander conquered. At its core this amounted to two things: the *Greek language* and the *Greek city*. Greek became the *lingua franca* of the Mediterranean, including Palestine. The importance of the advent of a common, international language cannot be exaggerated. It made not merely communication, but, in turn, trade, travel, politics, religion—indeed all of life different from what it had been before. The East and the West met in a manner that went beyond previous, distanced encounters through the medium of common language.

Hand in hand with the creative force of commonality of language went the establishment of a new way of life, *the city* (Greek, *polis*), styled on the model of the Greek cities Alexander and the Greeks cherished. These cities were planned and built to attract residents by making available to them experiences in living that went beyond the lifestyle available in rural and semi-rural settings. In the city there was the opportunity for cultural offerings in the city's institutions: the stadium, the gymnasium, theaters, and diverse temples. Moreover, a rich social life was possible, and residents had the opportunity to participate in more-or-less limited manners in the politics of the city. Educators were attracted to the cities, and they offered instruction in a variety of private and public settings. The cities were centers of organized trade, and as commerce thrived travel increased as goods were transported to city markets. Some of the most striking results of all this activity were large population shifts, extensive cultural and religious syncretism, and the emergence of a new, self-made, middle social class that established itself through the doing of business.

Luke and Acts reflect the glories of this Hellenistic world in a number of ways, small and big. The "tile" roof mentioned in Luke 5:19 is typical of an urban Hellenistic dwelling, not a rural Palestinian hut. The practice of "stewardship" (Luke 16:1-18; 19:11-27) evolved during the Hellenistic era. The travels of Paul in Acts were possible because of trade routes of the age, and the silver industry in Ephesus of which Luke writes in Acts 19 demonstrates how cities developed specialty crafts that presupposed extensive trading.[7]

There were also obvious, negative results to this process of Hellenistic urbanization. With the rise of the city came the slow, steady demise of rural life. Those with extensive land holdings let out their farms to tenants and moved to the city for a life of leisure. Coupled with this the political overlords usually levied heavy taxes on profits from agricultural production, and payment was generally taken out of the tenants' share of the profit. Thus those remaining in the country and doing the hard work of farm labor were heavily taxed and bilked of their earnings—in short, they were oppressed. It is no surprise therefore that the poor and uneducated migrated off the land and into the cities in search of a better life.

But the cities could not accommodate and support their ever burgeoning populations. The results were predictable: the cities were filled with beggars, and the countrysides were full of bandits. Smalltime revolts were a constant threat to stability of life, and an ancient form of *Angst* characterized the age. The historian, Gilbert Murray, refers to the late Hellenistic period as an age of failure of nerve;[8] and while this is an overstatement, it is true that ultimately the Hellenistic way of life led to a mood of questioning of the leaders, institutions (especially religious), and structure of society. People sought a variety of means for coping with their malaise. Some turned to religion. There was a loss of interest in the traditional state religions, but fascination with fate, astrology, numerology, magic, and a plethora of mystery religions, waxed vigorously. Others found the more logical means of coping offered by philosophy attractive. The Hellenistic schools of Epicurean, Cynic, Stoic, and (Neo-)Pythagorean philosophy found new adherents; and though true philosophy had no great impact on the masses, popularized forms of these movements did provide some direction for most of the population. Even Judaism enjoyed some appeal to the Hellenistic peoples. True, an anti-Jewish sentiment did color portions of the population, but many others were attracted to the sophistication of monotheism, the high moral standards of Judaism, and the appeal of a religion that offered a relationship to a personal God who chose a people and related to them through grace and the gift of the Law. While many could never bring themselves to convert to Judaism, they numbered themselves as "God-fearers" and had close and deep ties to the life of the synagogue.

Luke and Acts also reflect the tragic side of the Hellenized world of the first century. The story of the good Samaritan (Luke 10:30-37) presupposes the trade and travel *and* the bandits that characterized the time. The mention of Pilate's execution of rebellious Galileans (Luke 13:1-5) reflects political turmoil, as do the references to Roman taxation in Luke 20:20-26; 23:2. Above all, Luke 21:20-24 narrates with the precision of hindsight the destruction of Jerusalem in A.D. 70. Furthermore, one sees the vitality of "religions" as attempts to deal with the malaise of the era in the mentions of Simon the magician (Acts 8), a clairvoyant slavegirl (Acts 16), the religious syncretism and pluralism of Athens (Acts 17), and the Acts accounts of the establishment of Christian churches throughout the Mediterranean.

While Luke's world was thoroughly Hellenized, the Gospel according to Luke and much of Acts are set in a particularly *Jewish* portion of that larger world. This observation raises the further question, "What identified the 'average' Jew of Jesus' day and of the time of the early church?" At the time or about the time of Jesus' birth there were perhaps three to four and a half million Jews living around the Mediterranean. Approximately half a million Jews lived in Palestine.[9] There were 6,000 Pharisees, 4,000 Essenes, and a few hundred (certainly not even 1,000) Sadducees.[10] Thus the identifiable sectarian Jews were a tiny minority among the bulk of the Jews. How were these "regular" Jews identifiable? First, despite the deliberate, conscientious distancing of Jewish life from the world of Hellenism, there are remarkable signs of Jewish accommodation to the Hellenistic way of life. This is true of all the sources available to us from this time in the life of Judaism, including especially the Dead Sea Scrolls—the documents left to us by the hardest line of ancient hasidic resistance to acculturation to Hellenism. Moreover, the existence of the synagogue as a place of worship, social life, and education resulted from Judaism's interaction with the Hellenistic world. The office of "rabbi" which arose in the Hellenistic period is a Jewish form of the Hellenistic emphasis on teaching and learning. The translation of the Hebrew Bible into its Greek version, the Septuagint (abbreviated or symbolized as LXX), happened because many Jews not only had Greek as their first language but were incapable of using Hebrew in study and worship. And, perhaps, above all, the creation of the writings called "wisdom literature," a Jewish form of philosophy, testifies to the Hellenization of Judaism. Therefore, though one cannot directly consult primary historical sources concerning developments in Judaism during the first centuries of the Hellenistic period (330s through 170s B.C.), the form of Judaism encountered in the literature that follows that time attests to a dynamic process of cultural syncretism that affected even those who believed themselves to be resisting Hellenism.

Yet, still, what characterized a Jew in Jesus' day? Perhaps four things:[11] (1) *monotheism*, i.e., the belief in the God of Abraham; (2) *nationalism*, i.e., a conviction that the God of Abraham gave to Abraham's heirs the "promised land;" (3) *concern for the Law*, i.e., belief that part of God's covenant with Israel was the giving of the Law as the standard for life in the context of the covenant; and, (4) *an apocalyptic perspective on the world*, i.e., a conviction that the world was set in opposition to God and that God was about to intervene in behalf of God's rightful lordship and in redemption of God's chosen people. One encounters this kind of thought in Daniel; Ezekiel; the Dead Sea Scrolls; 1 Enoch; the gospel accounts of the preaching of both John the Baptist and Jesus; the early Christian cry "maranatha" and the early Christian concern with the coming of the Son of Man; Paul's letters; Revelation; and the later Jewish Bar Kokhba revolt.

Behind much that Luke says lies the religion and politics of his own day (A.D. 80s and 90s), and while he labors to relate the events of the earlier decades to his readers, Luke cannot escape the inevitable retrospective coloring of the times about which he tells from the vantage point of his own day. Thus one needs as much information as is possible about the world in which Luke lived, believed, and wrote so that one can understand with the utmost clarity what Luke is trying to communicate to his readers in his own special way. This essay has sketched briefly the outlines of the history and culture of that period, but for a thorough understanding of Luke-Acts one is well-advised to turn to more extensive scholarly treatments and, above all, to the primary sources available from the period.

"History and Culture in Luke-Acts"

From viewing the general historical and cultural setting in which Luke-Acts was produced it is well to turn to a consideration of telltale signs of Luke's world in the narrative he has crafted. The inclusion of certain data, sometimes items that Luke simply assumes and sometimes facts that he seems to know, gives the story a ring of authenticity and sets the story in the context of the first-century Mediterranean world. No attempt will be made here to determine whether this information is historical or verisimilar. In fact, careful analysis leads scholars to a variety of conclusions regarding the incidents in Luke-Acts: some reflect history, others are verisimilitude, and still others a bit of both. The purpose in this part of this essay is to identify a few of the phenomena of history and culture that Luke presupposes and includes in his narrative and, in turn, to ask how Luke's first readers are likely to have taken some of the information. Finally, we will consider what these items indicate about Luke as a citizen of the Greco-Roman world.

THE ENROLLMENT: LUKE 2:1-5

In Luke's Gospel this event is the motivation for the going of Joseph and Mary from Nazareth to Bethlehem where Jesus was born. Clearly Luke pursues theological ends with this narrative: worldwide history frames the birth of Jesus; Jesus does not come from a family of Jewish rebels—indeed his peace comes in the midst of the Pax Augusta, but supersedes it; Jesus' Davidic descent is made explicit, but the lowly estate of his birth defies the triumphalistic expectation of many Jews of the day and foreshadows the humiliation of his eventual death on the cross.

But, a first-century reader would have responded to the narrative with an even more nuanced comprehension. The imperial edict Luke describes would have listed and distinguished Roman citizens and the other inhabitants of the empire in the various provinces where they lived. Such censuses provided crucial information for military service and taxation.[12] An imperial edict applied only to imperial provinces, i.e., the provinces overseen by the emperor through the administrative services of his appointees, legates, proconsuls, and prefects— not to senatorial provinces. The imperial provinces were the more troubled portion of the empire, often regulated by government more nearly martial law than republican rule.[13] In this context censuses were not pleasant events, and they could threaten the fabric of the Pax Augusta.

THE CENTURION: LUKE 7:1-10

Luke tells the story of an exchange between a centurion (who never appears in the story himself) and Jesus. At its heart this pericope focuses on what constitutes religious *worthiness* and, in turn, what true faith looks like. Furthermore, this encounter anticipates the appearance of two other centurions in Luke-Acts, one at the cross who recognizes at the time and in the manner of Jesus' death that he was "righteous"[14] and the other, Cornelius, in Acts 10.

But, who was this man? An exact identification is impossible, but certainly the man is a Gentile (v. 9), and most likely he is a Roman, since the narrative portrays him in charge of a company of Roman soldiers (though there are other possibilities for interpretation).[15] Most important, however, he is a God-fearer.[16] God-fearers were Gentiles who were attached to Judaism's sophisticated monotheism, high moral standards, and system for maintaining one's righteousness through observance of the Law. These factors offered and enabled a kind of personal relation to God. Frequently what prevented God-fearers from becoming full converts (proselytes) to Judaism was circumcision. Aside from the physical discomfort to be associated with the act, certain social stigmata and liabilities ensued from undergoing the procedure. Therefore, the status of the God-fearers in relation to Jews was ambiguous. At times (as is the case in this story) they are highly regarded, but because they were uncircumcised, God-fearers were still considered to be unclean; and so, they were subject to discrimination within the context of the Jewish cultus and the life of the synagogue. Thus the centurion was a man who was marginalized on two fronts: his religious sensibilities made him unable to participate freely or fully in the culture and politics of the Roman world and his personal or social scruples prevented him from finding a true home in the life of the Jewish community. Behind whatever theological concerns operate in this story there may lie a fuller understanding of Luke the citizen of the first century and his readers. Despite the esteem in which the centurion is held, his liminal status regarding Judaism may have precluded his approaching Jesus directly because of uncertainty about the reception. In any case, the faith he demonstrates is even greater than is apparent from first study of the story. The centurion does not merely believe that Jesus *could heal from afar*; he believes that the power of God operative in the ministry of Jesus *would heal across the ethnic boundaries maintained by Judaism*—boundaries that affect his life on a daily basis and to which he simply should have grown accustomed.

JERUSALEM UNDER SIEGE: LUKE 21:5-7, 20-24

The Lukan version of the prophecy of Jesus about the destruction is noticeably more explicit in terms of detail than the parallel passages in Mark and Matthew. The consensus of scholars is that Luke filled out the statement from the vantage point of hindsight[17] and with reference to the LXX.[18] Comparison of Luke's version of the prophecy with the account by Josephus of the destruction of Jerusalem by Titus' army finds significant parallels, e.g., the mention of (a) camps surrounding Jerusalem, (b) the terrible plight of pregnant women during this time, (c) the Judaeans' and Jerusalemites' being put to the sword, (d) their being carried off as captives, and (e) the trampling of Jerusalem by Gentiles.[19]

One cannot determine with certainty whether Luke drew upon specific information concerning the destruction of Jerusalem or whether he filled out the prophecy from a general knowledge of what happened during such military sieges, or both. But, military tales, motifs, and metaphors were common in Luke's world; and the efficient destructive capacity of the Roman army was well-known. The details of the Lukan version of the prophecy would have stimulated a vivid image in the minds of Luke's readers, who would have had some knowledge of the war tactics of the Roman army.

THE LAST SUPPER: LUKE 22:14-38

This meal of Jesus with his disciples is one in a long series of meals that Luke narrates (see 5:29-39: 7:36-50; 9:12-17; 10:38-42; 11:37-52; 14:1-35; 24:28-31, 41-43 [?]). The extended dialogue between Jesus and his disciples in the context of the supper and the interpretation of the teaching of Jesus after the banquet meal in the framework of the supper distinguish this story from its Synoptic counterparts.

Scholars have frequently described Luke's version of the last supper as a *testamentary banquet*.[20] The literary genre of *testaments* is well attested in classical Greek literature;[21] the Old Testament, canonical[22] and apocryphal;[23] the pseudepigrapha;[24] the New Testament, canonical[25] and apocryphal.[26]

Although testamentary literature is common in antiquity, no binding genre was employed by the authors of the *testaments*. But, in studying the various examples of this literary type, one can discern a common, loose format:[27] the main character is an ideal figure. Recognizing a special time, usually his own impending death, the main figure calls together his family or followers. When they are assembled, the central figure gives them special instructions. He often speaks of his own fatal flaw, predicts the future for them, and admonishes and/or instructs them in the ways of righteousness. Luke's account clearly fits into this pattern.[28]

The main character in 22:14-38 is Jesus. Throughout the gospel, Jesus has been aware that he will die in a way related to his mission. In 22:14-38, Luke has Jesus speak openly about his impending death at least three times (vv. 15-18, 19-20, and 22). Moreover, the temporal references on the lips of Jesus at 18b and 36b suggest that a special time has arrived.

In this story Luke informs the reader that Jesus' disciples were present with Jesus at table during the last supper (v. 14). The instruction that Jesus gives his followers in the context of the last supper may be matched against the three topics mentioned as typical of testamentary teaching. First, the main character informs those around him of a fatal flaw. Since Luke thinks of Jesus as the "righteous" one (23:47), "a savior, who is Christ the Lord" (2:11), one should not be surprised that Jesus does not tell of a fatal flaw. Yet, one does find in the place of this type of information Jesus' announcing (22:31) that Satan is involved in his forthcoming passion and death. Second, the main testament given usually predicts the future for those around the ideal figure. In Luke Jesus opens the future by relating it to his imminent death. He is about to suffer (v. 15), but somehow his suffering moves toward the kingdom of God (vv. 16, 18). His death provides a basis for the disciples' remembrance of him (19f) and realizes the plan of God (v. 37). And, even though Jesus is slated to suffer and die, he can offer the disciples a portion of his own inheritance (vv. 28-30). Still, he must warn the apostles of the trials that they will face (vv. 31, 36), even though he has made provision for their ultimate triumph (v. 32). Third, the main testamentary character admonishes and instructs those around him in the ways of righteousness. Jesus prepares his disciples for the crisis ahead by giving them direction. He offers his passion as the foundation for their future actions (vv. 19-20) and gives precepts for community conduct (vv. 24-27). He reminds the twelve that he sent them on a mission and tells them to prepare for hardship as they continue in the same activity (vv. 35-36). Thus, Luke shapes the last supper in terms of a literary form that would have been intelligible to his readers. The form of the story would have cued the first-century reader on how they were to approach the text.

Acts has similar kinds of historical and cultural information.

THE INCIDENT AT LYSTRA: ACTS 14:8-(11)20

Lystra was a city in south central Asia Minor which during the first century was aligned politically as part of the Roman province of Galatia. Augustus constituted the city as a Roman colony, and so, the population was multilingual, speaking Latin, Greek, and the native Lycaonian.[29] In this story Luke tells of the outburst of the people of Lystra in the native dialect/language, Lycaonian. Luke probably mentions the eruption of the people in Lycaonian in order to explain through the vehicle of narrative why Paul and Barnabas did not immediately object to the accolades directed toward them—they did not understand what was being said.[30] In handling the storytelling in this manner, Luke creates a lifelike scene that reflects one of the realities of the Roman world. Despite the extensive, centuries old Hellenization of the eastern Mediterranean, the ancient regional dialects and languages survived in the everyday lives of the inhabitants of the regions, though official business and written communication were done in Greek or Latin. Strikingly, at the same time that Luke has Barnabas and Paul praised in Lycaonian, his story has the crowd call them Zeus and Hermes, names of Greek, not Lycaonian, gods. This seeming oddity or absurdity is, however, itself a fair reflection of the cultural realities of Luke's world.[31] The regions of Asia Minor (and much of the rest of the Roman empire) were highly syncretistic. Native populations frequently Hellenized their deities by taking over Greek names and fusing the characteristics of the foreign gods with those of similar ones of their own religion(s).

LYDIA OF PHILIPPI: ACTS 16:14-15, 40

In the story of Paul, Silas, and Timothy in Philippi (Acts 16:11-40), Luke narrates two brief incidents in which a woman named Lydia is mentioned. In this woman one meets a character that, if not a common figure in the Roman world, was at least a normal one.[32] Lydia was a well-to-do, God-fearing, independent business woman. She was of the merchant class, dealing in purple materials. Such goods were among the luxury items that rich people purchased in order to signal their status, success, and wealth. Most likely Lydia herself would have been wealthy, not only because of her trading in status-symbol merchandise, but as is indicated by her ability to house and host the transient Christian preachers. Like many ancient merchants, Lydia seems to have taken up residence in a city other than her hometown, Thyatira, a city of Asia Minor that specialized in the manufacture of purple dye. The location of Philippi as a seaport and along the Via Egnatia (a major Roman military highway) would have facilitated the necessary activities of a merchant. The independence of this non-Jewish woman is a far cry from the second-class status that normally characterized women in Jewish Palestine and in the rural areas of the larger Greco-Roman world. Lydia was an urbanite, and her person, in terms of independence and status, sums up the progressive attitudes and lifestyles of the large cities of Luke's world. In the context in which the reader of Acts encounters Lydia her demeanor is simply normal, but recall that in the context of the ministry of Jesus in Galilee and Judaea, Jesus' association with and acceptance of women into his band of disciples was thought to be something remarkable.[33] Luke knows, and apparently his readers would have understood, both contexts. Finally, while Lydia heard and believed the gospel (as a result of God's opening her heart!) and subsequently was baptized, her former religious status was that of a God-fearer, not a proselyte to Judaism. She could have converted by undergoing proselyte baptism and making an offering to God. The barrier of circumcision did not hinder the female Gentile from converting to Judaism. Luke does not relate why Lydia had not made the move to become officially Jewish, but an informed reader would at least comprehend that God moved her in relation to the gospel to do what she had not done before, viz., convert.

Particularly in relation to Paul's work in the most famous cities of the Roman world, Luke preserves images of the historical and cultural realities of his day. We shall consider a portion of what Luke discloses in relation to Athens.

PAUL AT ATHENS: ACTS 17:16-34

Luke tells of Paul's preaching in Athens in an extremely subtle way. He gives nuance to his narrative by presupposing specific historical and cultural realia, known to literate citizens of the first century but frequently unknown to later readers. A few items of information give the twentieth-century readers a new perspective on the story. For example, Athens was a small city of about 5,000 citizens during Paul's day,[34] and though the former glory was remembered, the days of real resplendence were gone.

Luke has Paul in Athens addressing two distinct groups, (1) the Jews and God-fearers in the synagogue and (2) the Gentiles in the marketplace.[35] This distinction is unique in the Lukan narrative, but in having Paul active on two fronts Luke casts him in a relation to the larger Gentile population that is similar to the manner in which the great Athenian philosopher Socrates taught.[36] While engaging in conversation with the people in the marketplace Paul comes to the attention of some Athenian philosophers. Luke tells the reader merely that "certain of the Epicurean and Stoic philosophers conferred with him, and some said, 'What in the world is this idle gossip trying to say?'; but others [said], 'He seems to be a propounder of foreign deities'" (v. 18). Luke does not need to tell his first-century readers that the former comment would have come from the Epicureans (known for materialism and practical atheism) and the latter remark from the Stoics.[37]

As the story unfolds, Luke, as narrator, informs his readers that "all the Athenians and the foreigners residing there had no time for anything other than talking or hearing about the latest novelty" (v. 21). This statement would have been no news to the first readers of Luke's text, for the curiosity of the residents of Athens was proverbial; indeed, in this remark one sees Luke playing to the popular prejudices of his audience in this caricature of the Athenians.[38]

Thus far in the story all Luke's characters are behaving exactly as one would expect, given the known history and culture of Athens. But, in what follows the developments are remarkable. Paul, behaving like Socrates, is called on by the philosophers of Athens to speak his piece. From the narrative the reader knows that some of these philosophers anticipate that they will hear about "foreign deities" from Paul. This situation would have been especially striking to Luke's first readers, and it becomes intriguing even today when one remembers that Socrates was tried and executed for introducing strange gods and perverting the youth.[39] With this information in mind, one better understands the situation in which Luke casts Paul. While Luke does not inform the reader that Paul is in danger (perhaps he was not), nevertheless, the first-century reader would have clearly understood that Paul was not merely engaging in a pleasant philosophical or theological debate, for the stakes in such exchanges in Athens were high. Moreover, instead of preaching the "latest novelty," Paul takes a shrewd line as he addresses his hearers[40]—he starts by referring to one of their own religious shrines, an altar "to the unknown god." In his proclamation Paul is unlike Socrates, for he advocates nothing new; rather he clarifies the identify of the creator God (a deity that the Stoics would have known about) and ultimately relates the God of creation (who also sustains the world) to the resurrection of Jesus (vv. 18, 31).

One often reads or hears about Paul's unsuccessful work in Athens, but in fact the response to Paul's preaching there is no different from the response in other situations in Acts; some mock, some want to hear more, and some (even certain named individuals) believe. The noticeable features of this story are not the levels of success or failure of Paul's preaching mission, but the way that Luke has shaped and colored his narrative in relation to the history and culture of Athens as first-century readers knew it.[41]

Conclusion

An enormous volume could be produced merely providing commentary on the historical and cultural information that Luke presupposes and implies in his two volumes. Indeed nearly, if not, every story is related to such information. This manner of writing makes Luke a good historian in his own period. Today we would describe his narrative as verisimilitude because of the amount of creativity that he exercises; but by the standards of the first century Luke was not so much taking liberties with the events he sought to narrate as he was following the conventions of history writing of his day.

Luke's writings show us that he was a cultured, relatively sophisticated citizen of his world. He is aware of cultural patterns from a variety of geographical regions. He shows familiarity with political, military, and social structures and institutions. He seems to assume a sophisticated audience with his finely nuanced narrative. Luke was no mere provincial, but rather a cosmopolitan believer who styled his story from and for an appreciation for subtlety.

3

Luke the Christian

Dennis M. Sweetland

There is unanimous agreement among scholars that the author of the Third Gospel and the Acts of the Apostles was a Christian. While most believe that Luke was a Gentile Christian,[1] some contend that he was a Jewish Christian.[2] This insight, that Luke was a Christian, is extremely important, because it is as a Christian that Luke approaches both the Jesus tradition, which he uses to create the gospel, and the early Christian lore which lie behind the Acts of the Apostles.

Luke believes that God, who is ultimately in control of his creation, has a plan by which human beings can gain eternal salvation. This plan, revealed by God in the Hebrew Scriptures in the form of prophecies, has been fulfilled in the life and ministry of Jesus Christ. The fact that these prophecies/promises have been fulfilled is presented by Luke as having been attested to by the apostles and other early Christian missionaries, who then invited their audience to repent and be baptized.

This being said, the remainder of this article will be divided into five parts. (1) A more detailed examination of Luke's theology, christology, and the divine plan will serve to highlight the important role of God in Luke-Acts. (2) These comments on God's plan will lead to a discussion of salvation history and soteriology, two areas of Lukan theology where much scholarly debate has taken place. (3) The fact that God's gift of salvation is universal, according to Luke, will require an examination of the witness theme, and of the place of the Jews and of the marginalized in the divine plan. (4) The need of those who would be saved both to seek God and to accept God's offer of salvation requires a few words on Christian discipleship. (5) A final section will summarize the main points of the article.

* Notes for Chapter 3 can be found on pp. 168-71

1. God's Plan

LUKE'S THEOLOGY AND CHRISTOLOGY

Luke is able to assure his readers that salvation has been made available to human beings because he presents the one who offers this salvation as ultimately in control of events both in heaven and on earth. The third evangelist seems to depend primarily on the portrait of God in the Hebrew Scriptures as he presents his readers with the picture of a God who exercises sovereign control over history.[3] He emphasizes the supremacy of God when he describes God as both the Savior (Luke 1:47) and the "Soverign Lord" *despotēs)* who made "the heaven and the earth and the sea and everything in them" (Acts 4:24; cf. Luke 2:29).[4]

In Luke's understanding, however, the "Lord of heaven and earth" (Luke 10:21) also cares personally for humanity and takes an active part in the history of salvation. God, who has been at work (directing, leading, planning) throughout the history of Israel, entered human history in order to show his mercy (1:72, 78; 6:36) and to bring salvation to human beings. God's numerous visits during the history of Israel culminate in his visitation to Israel in the person of Jesus (7:16; Acts 15:14), who proclaims God's mercy (cf. Luke 10:37; 15:1-32) and offers salvation to all human beings (3:6; 19:10).

The loving, caring God (cf. Luke 6:35; 11:13) one encounters in Luke-Acts is the God of Israel (1:68ff.; cf. Acts 3:13; 5:30; 22:14) and the Father of Jesus (cf. Luke 10:21-22; 22:29; 23:46; 24:49) and of his disciples (cf. 6:36; 11:2; 12:30-32). He is the one who controls human events and takes the initiative in calling all to salvation. Although human beings, both Jews (Luke 11:9) and Gentiles (Acts 15:17), have to seek God in order to find God,[5] he is never far away (cf. Acts 14:17; 17:27).

God's plan for the salvation of all humanity includes the proclamation of salvation by Jesus during his earthly ministry and the proclamation about Jesus, the resurrected and exalted one, by the early church. The person and activity of Jesus Christ are at the center of Lukan theology because "there is salvation in no one else" (Acts 4:12).[6] Luke presents Jesus of Nazareth as a human being (Luke 2:6-7; Acts 2:22) who acts as God's agent in bringing the gift of salvation to humanity. Jesus shows mercy and compassion in his active concern for "the poor, the maimed, the lame, the blind" (Luke 14:13; cf. 4:18), sinners (5:30; 7:34; 15:1), and other outcasts (5:12-16; 10:25-37; 17:11-19). There are things about this special emissary of God, however, that serve to set him apart from others. Jesus is conceived through the power of the Holy Spirit (1:34-35), resurrected from the dead (e.g., 24:6; Acts 2:24, 32), and has ascended to God's right hand (Acts 2:33; 5:31; cf. 1:9).

The third evangelist also presents Jesus as acting with divine authority. He is the only Synoptic evangelist to use the title "Savior" (*sōtēr*), a title used for God in the Hebrew Scriptures (Isaiah 45:21), for Jesus (Luke 2:11; cf. Acts 5:31; 13:23).[7] Luke is obviously aware of the Hebrew tradition since Mary refers to God as "my Savior" in her Magnificat (Luke 1:47). In applying the same title to God and Jesus, Luke is emphasizing that God has made salvation available in Jesus (Acts 4:12).

The title "Lord" (*kyrios*) is the most frequently used title for Jesus in Luke-Acts.[8] As he did with "Savior," Luke also applies the title "Lord" to both God (e.g., Luke 1:6ff.; 19:38; 20:42; Acts 3:20; 7:31ff.) and Jesus (e.g., Luke 1:43; 2:11; 24:34; Acts 1:6, 21; 2:36). The dominion, power, and authority that God and Jesus are said to exercise over human beings is emphasized by Luke's use of "Lord" (*kyrios*).

Luke also uses the traditional titles "Messiah" or "Christ," "Son of God" and "Son of Man" to refer to Jesus. The title "Messiah" or "Christ" (*christos*) is a comprehensive term which identifies Jesus as God's final, supreme agent in the history of salvation (Luke 2:26; 9:20). Often seen as the most important title for Jesus in Luke-Acts, *christos* would have suggested both royalty ("king") and Davidic descent ("Son of David"). The first identification of Jesus in the gospel is provided when the angel Gabriel informs Mary that her son Jesus will be called the Son of God (1:32-35).[9] The angel's words are confirmed at the transfiguration when God, referring to Jesus, says, "This is my Son, my Chosen, listen to him!" (9:35). At his baptism, the heavenly voice identifies Jesus as "my beloved Son" (3:22). It seems clear that Luke uses the title "Son of God" to focus on the unique filial relationship between Jesus and God.

The title "Son of God," like "Lord" and "Savior," serves to highlight the power and authority now exercised by the risen Christ. Those who focus exclusively on power and glory, however, miss an extremely important aspect of Lukan christology, suffering messiahship. Luke clearly believes that anyone who wishes to know Jesus must understand him as the suffering, dying Messiah. The risen Jesus reminds his disciples on two occasions that a correct understanding of messiahship must include suffering and death, as well as resurrection (Luke 24:25-27, 44-46; cf. Acts 3:18; 17:3; 26:23). In order to emphasize this motif, Luke has included in the gospel sayings about the suffering Son of Man and has deliberately portrayed Jesus as the suffering servant of Isaiah 40-55.

While Luke uses the title "Son of Man" both to refer to Jesus' earthly ministry and to his future coming in glory or judgment, our primary interest lies in those "Son of Man" sayings which refer to the passion.[10] Relying for the most part on Mark and Q, Luke identifies Jesus as the Son of Man who will be delivered into the hands of "men" and Gentiles (Luke 9:44; 18:32; 22:22; 24:7), to be killed, and be raised (9:22; 18:33; 24:7). These sayings highlight an important aspect of Lukan christology and have profound implications for Christian discipleship. Jesus, the Messiah, Lord and Savior, is also the suffering Son of Man. As such, he becomes a model for the suffering and persecution that his disciples endure (cf. Luke 6:22; Acts 7:56).[11] This theme is amplified by Luke's portrayal of Jesus as the Isaian suffering servant.[12]

Once Luke has established that God exercises active control over everything in heaven and on earth, he must explain to the reader exactly how this Sovereign Lord has made salvation available to human beings. To this end Luke presents his belief that God had a plan for the salvation of human beings which was worked out in the history of Israel, Jesus, and the early church. As the central figure in God's plan, Jesus of Nazareth unifies past, present, and future. He is the one who was promised in the Jewish Scriptures, is God's primary agent in bringing salvation to humanity, and continues to perform this task after his resurrection and ascension through his selected representatives in the early church.

GOD'S PLAN REVEALED IN THE HEBREW SCRIPTURES

Luke believes that there is a divine plan for the salvation of human beings which has been revealed by God in the Hebrew Scriptures. This is seen in the gospel, where we read that the Pharisees and the lawyers rejected God's purpose or plan (*boulē*) for themselves, because they were not baptized by John (Luke 7:30), and in Acts, where Peter announces to his audience at Pentecost that Jesus was "delivered up according to the definite plan (*boulē*) and foreknowledge of God" (Acts 2:23; cf. Acts 20:27; 13:36). Luke also tells his readers that God has predetermined certain things to take place. In the gospel, Jesus says that "the Son of Man goes as it has been determined" (Luke 22:22). In Acts, the reader learns that Jesus has been "ordained by God to be judge of the living and the dead" (Acts 10:42; cf. 17:31) and that Paul's conversion is part of God's plan (22:14; 26:16).

Further evidence that the third evangelist believes a divine plan was at work in the history of Israel, Jesus, and the early church is seen in Luke's use of the impersonal verb *dei*. Widely recognized as Luke's favorite term to express necessity, *dei* denotes compulsion of any kind[13] and is usually translated as "it is necessary" or "must."[14] Among the numerous things that are necessary, the Lukan Jesus mentions the fulfilment of all that was written about him in the Law of Moses and the prophets (Luke 24:44), especially the suffering, death, and resurrection of the Son of Man (9:22). Acts confirms that Scripture had to be fulfilled (Acts 1:16; cf. 3:21); Jesus had to suffer and rise from the dead (17:3); and Paul had to suffer for the sake of Jesus' name (9:16) and bear witness about Jesus at Rome (23:11; cf. 27:24). Therefore, Luke believes that the time of the church, as well as the ministry of Jesus, is guided by God.

PROMISES FULFILLED IN JESUS

Luke is in agreement with the basic conviction of the Hebrew Scriptures when he portrays God as present in the historical struggle, directing the course of human events toward his own end. What is uniquely Christian in Luke's presentation is his claim that the promises of God have been fulfilled in the life, death, and resurrection of Jesus and in the life of the early Christian community.[15] This motif, the fulfilment of prophecy, is a major theme in Luke-Acts and, like the saving activity of God, serves as a link between the testaments.

The career of Jesus as a whole, as well as numerous specific parts of that ministry, is seen in Luke-Acts as the fulfilment of earlier prophecy. Luke tells his readers that Jesus entered the synagogue at Nazareth, read from Isaiah (61:1-2; 58:6), and then said, "Today this scripture has been fulfilled in your hearing" (Luke 4:21). At the end of the gospel, Jesus tells his disciples "that everything written about me in the law of Moses and the prophets and the psalms must be fulfilled" (24:44-46) and "beginning with Moses and all the prophets, he interpreted to them in all the scriptures the things concerning himself" (24:27). While prophecies found in Isaiah play an extremely important role in Luke-Acts (e.g., Luke 4:16-21; cf. 7:22f. and 9:35), it should be noted that as part of his "proof from prophecy" theme Luke also cites both the prophets as a whole (e.g., Luke 18:31; Acts 3:18; 13:27) and specific prophecies found in Malachi (3:1; 4:5-6; cf. Luke 1:13-17), Micah (5:2; cf. Luke 2:4), Joel (Acts 2:16-21), Amos (Acts 14:15f.), 2 Samuel (7:9-14; cf. Luke 1:30-33), the Psalms (Psalm 2; cf. Acts 4:25 and Psalm 118; cf. Luke 20:17f.), and Deuteronomy (18:15f.; cf. Acts 3:22f.). Luke believes that, in agreement with God's design, these earlier prophecies have been fulfilled in the ministry of Jesus and the early church.

Among the many prophecies Jesus fulfils, according to Luke, is the promise of God to raise up a prophet like Moses in the last days (Acts 3:22-23; cf. Deut 18:15-16, 19; Lev 23:29). Jesus is considered to be a prophet by many of his contemporaries (Luke 9:18-19; cf. 7:16) and identifies himself as a prophet (13:33). He makes numerous predictions in the course of his ministry, most of which come to pass later on in the narrative.

His announcement in the synagogue at Nazareth that the Isaiah prophecy has been fulfilled (Luke 4:21) is also a prediction about his own ministry which is about to begin. This prediction is fulfilled (cf. 7:21-22) as are his predictions of his passion (9:22, 44; 18:31-33; cf. 22:24), his prediction of Peter's denial (22:34; cf. 22:54-61), and his prophecy that the Father will give the Holy Spirit to those who ask him (11:13; cf. Acts 2:1ff.).

In Luke's story some predictions of Jesus are not fulfilled during his earthly existence. Jesus predicts that the temple will be destroyed (Luke 13:35; 21:6), that Jerusalem will be captured by Gentiles (19:43-44; 21:20-24; 23:28-31), and that the good news will be preached to the Gentiles (24:47; Acts 1:8). Readers of Luke-Acts, however, would have known that these predictions had been fulfilled in the events of 70 A.D. and in the success of the Gentile mission. Some predictions involving eschatological events remain unfulfilled (e.g., Luke 1:33; 9:24-27; 12:8-10; Acts 1:11). Because numerous predictions of Jesus find their fulfilment within the narrative, the reader is led to see Jesus' predictions as reliable and to expect that these eschatological predictions will be fulfilled as well.

Luke clearly presents God as being in soverign control of all creation. This loving, caring God has a plan for the salvation of human beings which he has revealed in the Jewish Scriptures (e.g., Isaiah 25:9; 26:18; 45:17; 61:1). Luke believes that these promises of God have been realized in the ministry of Jesus (e.g., Luke 4:18-21; 7:22), God's Messiah, and that this salvation will be proclaimed by the early Christian missionaries (Acts 4:12; 13:46-47) who, like Jesus, are instruments in God's plan.

2. Current Debate Regarding Luke's Theology

SALVATION HISTORY

How does Luke's understanding of God's plan affect his understanding of human history? The scholarly debate about Luke's conception of salvation history has centered on two issues during the past half century: (1) the timetable for the parousia, therefore Luke's eschatology, and (2) the number of stages or phases in Lukan salvation-history. Most influential in both these areas has been the work of H. Conzelmann.[16]

Conzelmann claims that Luke has relegated the parousia to

a remote and indefinite future. The expectation of the imminent return of Jesus, which Luke found in Mark's Gospel and in the other traditional material available to him, would have run into trouble with the passage of time. Luke's solution, according to Conzelmann, was to abandon all hope for the early return of Jesus and to portray Jesus and the church as expecting the parousia only in the far distant future. For the expectation of an imminent parousia, Luke substituted the claim that history was being worked out in stages in accordance with God's plan.[17]

Few scholars would defend Conzelmann's position today.[18] What has been pointed out on numerous occasions is: (1) that Luke has retained a number of traditional sayings about an imminent judgment (Luke 3:7-17) or an imminent coming of the Son of Man (21:27, 32) or the kingdom (10:9) and (2) that Luke has added to this traditional material sayings about the imminent coming of the kingdom (10:11; 21:31) or judgment (18:7-8).[19] The best conclusion, therefore, is that Luke has not completely abandoned the traditional belief that the parousia would take place in the near future.[20] If Luke has downplayed or subordinated the eschatological emphasis in some of the traditional material at his disposal and has shown less interest in the expectation of the parousia in Acts,[21] it is primarily because of his pastoral concerns. Luke's shift of emphasis results in the reader focusing more on the presence of Jesus, the risen Lord, and less on his future return, more on Jesus' life and ministry as a guide for Christian conduct and less on the motivating force of an imminent judgment.

There still seems to be some disagreement, however, concerning the number of stages or phases in Lukan salvation history. Conzelmann's thesis, that Luke has a three-stage view of salvation-history (the time of Israel, the time of Jesus, and the time of the church), has evoked widespread scholarly response. Although few today adopt Conzelmann's model without question, some continue to accept various modified versions of his three-stage model.[22] Others, however, believe that Luke is working with a two-stage understanding of salvation-history. Those who adopt the second position agree that Luke divides the time of Jesus from the time of Israel, but they suggest that the model Luke is using is one of prophecy and fulfilment and that the time of Jesus and the time of the church are one.[23] Proponents of the two-stage model argue that Jesus was not the center, but the climax of God's salvation history.[24]

It is clear to both groups of scholars that Luke wants to stress the continuity between Israel, Jesus, and the church. Prior to his baptism, Jesus is seen by Luke as a figure in the period of Israel. There is also an obvious continuity between Jesus and the church. Luke sees both the ministry of Jesus and the time of the church as eschatological. The Spirit is at work and salvation is being offered to human beings both during the ministry of Jesus and in the preaching and missionary activity of the early church. Jesus is not a hero of the past, but the Lord of the present. As risen Lord, Jesus continues to be present to his community in word and sacrament.[25] What Jesus proclaimed about himself and the kingdom of God is now proclaimed by the early church in Acts and by Luke himself in his two-volume work.

SOTERIOLOGY

Conzelmann's conclusion that Luke understands history to be divided into three stages led him to claim that just as the eschaton was an event relegated to the far distant future by Luke, so too was eternal life "removed into the distance."[26] He also claimed that there is no "soteriological significance drawn from Jesus' suffering or death."[27] Although both these positions found early supporters, they have been challenged by recent scholarship.

Many scholars today argue that Luke does, in fact, have a theology of the cross. Luke has not eliminated the soteriological significance of the cross, but has added material from his sources to explain Jesus' death as part of God's design. God's plan for universal salvation included the death of Jesus, who was saved because of his faith and obedience (Luke 22:42; 23:46)[28] and whose resurrection-ascension makes universal salvation possible.[29]

There is also a scholarly consensus that salvation is available "today" and not in the far distant future as Conzelmann suggested.[30] It is often pointed out that Luke, in the gospel, has included many examples of the imminence of salvation. The shepherds in the field are told by the angels that a Savior is born to them "this day in the city of David" (Luke 2:11). After reading the saving prophecies of Isaiah, Jesus announces that "today this scripture has been fulfilled in your hearing" (4:21). It is "today" that sins are forgiven (5:26) and "today" that demons are cast out (13:32). Jesus tells Zacchaeus that "today salvation has come to this house" (Luke 19:9; cf. 19:5, Acts 26:29). And he says to the repentant thief, "Today you will be with me in paradise" (Luke 23:43).

The scholarly consensus, therefore, has moved away from Conzelmann's position on both Lukan soteriology and Lukan eschatology. It is now recognized that Luke has a theology of the cross and believes that salvation is available in the present. Because of the cross, salvation is now available through the activity of the Spirit within the Christian community.

3. *Universal Salvation*

'WE ALL ARE WITNESSES'

Because Luke believes that there is salvation in no one else except Jesus Christ of Nazareth (Acts 4:12) and because he believes that God wills this salvation be made available to all, a universal mission is required. This universal mission is fore-shadowed by the travels of Jesus himself as he fulfils his role of preaching the good news (Luke 4:34), and by Jesus' sending out of the twelve (9:1-6) and the seventy (10:1ff.). The importance of the universal mission becomes obvious in Acts 1:8 when the risen Lord tells his disciples that they shall be his "witnesses in Jerusalem and in all Judea and Samaria and to the end of the earth." According to Luke, once the mission begins it is the power of Jesus that enables these early Christian missionaries to be successful (e.g., Acts 3:12, 16; 4:7-12) as they preach the kingdom of God (Acts 8:12; 19:8; 20:25; 28:23, 31) in accordance with God's plan. It is the task of the Christian missionary to show potential disciples that the promises of God in the Hebrew Scriptures have been fulfilled in the life, death, and resurrection of Jesus (Acts 8:26-40; cf. Luke 24:27).

Acts is dominated by the theme of "witness."[31] Jesus commissions the apostles to be his witnesses (Acts 1:8) and it is said that the one chosen to replace Judas will become a witness to the resurrection of Jesus (1:22). Frequently we find the Christian missionaries Peter (2:32; 3:15; 10:39-41; cf. 5:29-32) and Paul (13:30-31; 22:14-15, 20; cf. 20:21, 24; 23:11) claiming that they are witnesses. Luke tells the Jesus story in such a way that those who will later be called witnesses are with Jesus for virtually his entire ministry. They witness his marvelous deeds and hear and understand his public teaching. In this way Luke seeks to guarantee the accuracy of the entire career of Jesus, from the baptism of John to the ascension (1:21-22; cf. Luke 1:1-4; Acts 1:1-5). Luke also wants to inform his readers that the gift of salvation is being offered to those who are outside the Israel of old.

The mission to the Gentiles, in which repentance and forgiveness of sins should be preached (Luke 24:47), is in complete agreement with God's plan (cf. Acts 14:16) as announced in the Hebrew Scriptures. Simeon cites Isaiah 49:6 when he identifies Jesus as "a light for revelation to the Gentiles" (Luke 2:32). Luke indicates that the Gentile mission was foreshadowed in Isaiah's prophecy (Isaiah 40:4-5) that "all flesh shall see the salvation of God" (Luke 3:4-6; cf. Mark 1:2-3). In Acts 15:16ff. James argues that Amos 9:11f. has been fulfilled in God's visitation to the Gentiles.

The role that the missionaries of the early church will play in God's plan is seen clearly when Paul says that Christ, being the first to rise from the dead, "would proclaim light both to the people and to the Gentiles" (Acts 26:22-23). The way in which Jesus, as risen Lord, proclaims this light to Jews and Gentiles is through the preaching of his missionary community.

LUKE AND THE JEWS

Scholars have long been interested in trying to understand the attitude of Luke, the Christian evangelist, toward Judaism. The difficulty is that the third evangelist presents both positive and negative statements about Judaism.[32] On the one hand, Luke has a very positive attitude toward both the Law and the temple.[33] It has even been claimed that for Luke "Christianity is true Pharisaism."[34] On the other hand, Luke severely criticizes the Jews for their refusal to accept Jesus and his gospel. When the Messiah arrived in fulfilment of God's promises both he and his gospel were rejected by most Jews. Does this widespread rejection of Jesus by the Jews mean that God has rejected them? Does God's plan include the complete rejection of Israel after the mission to the Gentiles has begun?

Using Acts 13:46; 18:3; and 28:28 in particular, many would argue that Luke has abandoned the hope of converting Israel and that he understands the Christian mission to be directed exclusively to the Gentiles.[35] They conclude that "Luke saw the reception of the Gentiles and the Gentile mission as being the result of the Jews' rejection of the gospel."[36] The promises which were fulfilled in Christ belong to Israel; but because Israel has been completely rejected, Luke must see the church as the new Israel.

Others argue that, according to Luke-Acts, the children of Abraham have not been completely rejected. "Luke knows that the mission to the Jews was a mixed success and is at a stalemate; however, in his composition he is careful to note that the mission to Israel is open-ended."[37] Both the blindness of the Jews (cf. Isa 6:9-10) and the listening of the Gentiles (cf. Ezek 3:6) are part of God's plan as foretold in the Hebrew Scriptures (Acts 28:26-28). But this does not mean that God has permanently rejected the Jews. The ignorance or blindness of Israel leads not to unforgiving condemnation and abandonment, but to the call for repentance. After all, God exalted Jesus "at his right hand as Leader and Savior, to give repentance to Israel and forgiveness of sins," (5:31). According to God's plan, the gift of salvation continues to be offered to all, Jews as well as Gentiles (Luke 24:46-47; Acts 2:32-39; 3:13-21; 5:31; 10:42-43; 11:18; 13:26-39).

Both the rejection and the acceptance of the gospel are seen by Luke as components of the divine plan of God revealed in the Jewish Scriptures. As early as the prophetic speech of Simeon (Luke 2:29-35), the mission to the Gentiles, as well as the mission to Israel, is seen as part of the divine plan. Luke's familiarity with the Jewish Scriptures has caused him to see the salvation of the Gentiles as a necessary part of the eschato-

logical action of God.[38] The risen Lord announces that "repentance and forgiveness of sins should be preached in his name
to all nations" (Luke 24:47), a theme which is found throughout Acts (e.g., Acts 3:25; 13:47; 15:16ff.).

THE MARGINALIZED

No discussion of universalism would be complete without
mentioning Luke's attitude toward the marginalized. The third
evangelist presents Jesus as especially concerned with tax collectors, sinners, the poor, and women. Although the job of tax
collector was considered a despicable occupation by first-century Judaism,[39] Jesus associates freely with them (Luke 5:29-
30; 7:29, 34; 15:1; cf. 18:9-14). In fact, the famous tax collectors
Levi (Luke 5:27-32) and Zacchaeus (19:1-10) are clearly numbered among Jesus' disciples. While association with sinners
was something to be avoided according to the Pharisees, Luke
presents Jesus as operating on a different principle. Jesus does
not ignore and avoid sinners, rather he associates with them
(e.g., 7:36-50; cf. 6:32-34) seeking the lost (15:1-32) in an effort
to bring them to repentance (5:32).

Luke's belief that salvation is universal is also found in
Jesus' association with women. The inferior status of women
in the Jewish society of Jesus' day and in late first-century
Judaism is well known.[40] Even in the wider Greco-Roman
world in which Luke writes, women do not enjoy the same
privileges that men enjoy. In Luke-Acts, however, the picture
is different. It is widely recognized that in Luke's two-volume
work stories about a man are frequently paralleled by stories
about a woman.[41] Women, at least one of whom is married,
are pictured as providing for Jesus and the twelve "out of their
means" (Luke 8:1-3). Women (4:39; 8:3; 10:40) as well as men
(Acts 6:2; 19:22) follow the example of Jesus (Luke 22:26f; cf.
12:37) and serve (*diakoneō*). Women speak prophetically (Acts
21:8-9) and function as missionaries (18:18, 26). In suggesting
that an equality exists between men and women, Luke the
Christian is more progressive than his Jewish or Greco-Roman
contemporaries.

Luke understands that God has made salvation available to

all through Jesus Christ. His favorable portrayal of women supports this in two ways. First, the universalism of salvation is suggested by the fact that the gospel is available to all without regard to gender. Luke shows his readers that women received the good news and helped to promote it in the church. Second, as we have seen above, Jesus came to seek and save the lost, the disadvantaged, the marginalized. One cannot ignore the fact that in first-century Israel women, as well as tax collectors, sinners, and the poor, were among society's marginalized. By presenting Jesus' association with women in such a positive light, whether they symbolize half of society because of their gender or more than half of society because of their social status, Luke has clearly shown that he believes that the gift of salvation is universal.

4. Christian Discipleship

REPENTANCE AND BELIEF

As Luke tells the story, early in his ministry Jesus announces that he has come to call sinners to repentance (Luke 5:32). Repentance (*metanoia*) involves a radical conversion from all that is evil and a total commitment to God. It is obvious that this call for conversion is not limited to the time of Jesus' earthly mission. The risen Lord tells his disciples that repentance and forgiveness of sins should be preached in his name to all nations (24:47). In Acts, a call to repentance and conversion usually forms an integral part of the missionary sermons.

The repentance spoken of in Luke-Acts is more than an intellectual exercise. Repentance involves belief or faith, but "faith" (*pistis*) implies obedience, as well as trust, hope, and the acceptance of the "good news."[42] One must actively strive to do the will of God. In the sermon on the plain, Jesus tells the readers of Luke's Gospel that those who hear his words must also incorporate them into their lives (Luke 6:46). This same theme appears later in the gospel, when Jesus identifies his true family as "those who hear the word of God and do it" (8:21), and when Jesus responds to the woman who praises his mother by pronouncing as blessed "those who hear the word of God and keep it" (11:28).

Faith is the proper response to the word of God (Luke 1:20; Acts 4:4; 15:7). Those who have faith in the "Lord Jesus" will be saved (Acts 16:31; cf. Luke 7:50) as they listen to the words of the "Lord" and act upon them (Luke 6:46; cf. 13:22-30). The resurrection and ascension of Jesus confirm that God's plan has been carried through; he has fulfilled his promises. The Christian should have faith in God, and in the one he raised from the dead, and live a life in accordance with God's will. One discovers the will of God in the words and deeds of Jesus, God's primary agent in the history of salvation (cf. Luke 6:46-49), and in the Spirit-guided missionary preaching of the early church.

ECCLESIOLOGY

It is clear that Luke expects those who confess Jesus as Lord and Savior to live an organized and communal way of life. And baptism appears to be the way in which the believer is incorporated into the Christian community Luke calls the church. While for Luke the existence of the Christian community is related to the words and deeds of Jesus, its emergence as a historical reality is associated with the pentecost event and the beginnings in Jerusalem.[43] After the Holy Spirit comes upon the assembled group of disciples at Pentecost, the church is equipped for its task of witness and mission. Salvation now becomes available "through the community of believers, in whose midst the Spirit is at work."[44] What is less clear is the exact structure of this early Christian community.

Most scholars agree that in Acts Luke presents his readers with three different structural models of the church: (1) the idealized Jerusalem community, (2) the community which is centered around Antioch and its missionary activity, and (3) the community which is reflected in Paul's speech to the Ephesian elders (Acts 20:18ff.).[45] As Luke narrates the evolution and growth of this community,[46] which is directed by the Spirit, different church structures emerge. The structure of the church, therefore, is seen as flexible and variable.

Luke knows no purely individualistic Christianity; therefore,

it appears as though he views some kind of church structure as indispensable. Exactly what that structure should be is not clear. Regardless of the structure of these communities, Luke understands that salvation comes to human beings through the missionary preaching of the church. In God's plan, salvation is through Christ whose word is committed to "the church of the Lord" (Acts 20:28).

5. Conclusion

The author of the Third Gospel and the Acts of the Apostles was a Christian theologian who wrote his two-volume work as a believer and for believers. When Luke glanced backward across the ages that preceded him, he did not see disorder and chaos, random events and happenings. As he looked at the history of the world, Luke saw a meaningful and carefully laid out plan of God unfolding before his eyes.

The one God, who created the universe, had revealed his plan for the salvation of human beings to the Hebrew people during nearly two thousand years of interaction with them. While this plan of God is found in the Jewish Scriptures, it is not immediately obvious to all. Luke believes that one needs a trustworthy guide in order to see the important parts of the plan and how these promises have been fulfilled in the life-death-resurrection of Jesus Christ. In the gospel, Luke informs the reader that Jesus himself led his first disciples to understand how he had fulfilled the earlier prophecies. In Acts, the reader sees how the early missionaries led those whom they encountered to see that Jesus had fulfilled the Jewish prophecies in his life, death, and resurrection. And Luke is providing the same helpful guidance to his readers.

Luke's life was different than it might have been because of his belief in Jesus and in what God has accomplished in Jesus Christ. Luke believes that the plan of God for the salvation of the world has been fulfilled. He and the Christian community to which he writes are living in the final days. Now is the time of salvation; now is the time to repent, to believe in the good news, and be baptized. Now is the time to rejoice and praise God for the salvation he has made available in Jesus Christ. Now is the time to reform one's life and begin to live in accordance with the will of God.

PART II

Methodological and Exegetical Studies

4

An Example of Rhetorical Criticism: Luke 4:16-30

Judette M. Kolasny

Historical criticism of the bible, or the historical-critical method, is concerned with the value of the biblical texts as evidence for reconstructing the history which they reflect, and for which they serve as documents.[1] This method has developed into an academic tradition consisting of a complex of traditional methods and solutions, and has become the fundamental scientific paradigm of biblical studies.[2] Recently, however, the historical-critical paradigm has been questioned.[3] Both form criticism and redaction criticism focus very much upon the individual pericope and tend to lose sight of the context in which the particular pericope is found. What is needed is a method which goes beyond these traditional forms: to look at the text as we have it; to look at the unified results and how it would be perceived by a group of near contemporaries.

In 1968, in his presidential address to the Society of Biblical Literature, James Muilenburg called upon biblical scholars to go beyond form criticism and look at passages of scripture in the context in which they are found.[4] He called this method "rhetorical criticism" and described it as:

> understanding the nature of Hebrew literary composition, ... exhibiting the structural patterns that are employed for the fashioning of a literary unit.... Such an enterprise I should describe as rhetoric and the methodology as rhetorical criticism.[5]

Although Muilenburg describes his method in application to a study of the Old Testament, efforts to apply this method to

---

* Notes for Chapter 4 can be found on pp. 171-72

New Testament studies have begun to emerge in recent years.[6]

In this study, the method as described above, will be used on a group of texts in Luke-Acts suggested by Norman Peterson's *Literary Criticism for New Testament Critics.*[7] Peterson suggests there are six pericopes in Luke-Acts having a common pattern and a theme of confrontation and rejection.[8] According to Peterson, Luke uses these pericopes as a literary device in his narrative and does so in order to accomplish one of his purposes, i.e., to show that Christianity emerged from and was the legitimate successor of Judaism.

In general, each of the pericopes reports a confrontation between an accredited agent of God (Jesus, Peter and Paul) and the people of God in their synagogues or temple. The confrontation results in the rejection of the agent by the people of God, followed by a forward movement of the agent and the continuation of the plan of God ultimately beyond the traditional people and holy places.[9] Because the scope of this study is limited, we will do a detailed analysis of only one of the texts (Luke 4:16-30), but the discussion will include its relationship to the other five. Basically, the question posed and which I attempt to answer is: how do pericopes of confrontation and rejection function in the Luke-Acts narrative?

Luke 4:16-30 As a Patterned Pericope

Each of the six stories follow this scheme: an opening action, interruption, a second action which in some sense continues the opening action, rejection, and an expansion element. In our analysis of Luke 4:16-30 we will first apply the pattern and then discuss its meaning and function.

1. PATTERN

a. Opening action (4:16-21): Jesus goes to the synagogue in Nazareth and stands to read from the scroll of Isaiah, after which he says: "Today this scripture has been fulfilled in your hearing" (4:21).

b. Interruption (4:22): Jesus' action is interrupted by a statement about the people's awe and marveling.

c. Second action (4:23-27): Jesus continues to speak, giving the examples of Elijah and Elisha, two prophets who did not minister to their own people, but to Gentiles.[10] Jesus' words are not only a response to the action of the people in the synagogue, but also a confrontation.

d. Rejection (4:28-29): All (*pantes*) in the synagogue, take offense at Jesus' words, probably because they recognized themselves as a people who throughout history had rejected God's agents. Jesus is rejected by the people and they attempt to kill him.

e. Extension or forward movement (4:30): Jesus escapes by passing through the crowd. He is able to continue his work.

Thus, Jesus preaches (first action), crowd reacts (interruption), Jesus continues his preaching (second action), and this leads to wrath and rejection on the part of the crowd. Because he escapes the crowd, the work of God's agent continues.

2. MEANING AND FUNCTION

The Nazareth pericope is a very important one because of its programmatic nature.[11] It is, so to speak, Jesus' inaugural address. In the Lukan version of the story of Jesus, it is Jesus' first public words. This pericope stands at the beginning of the Galilean ministry. This episode, however, is not the first time Jesus ministers, since Luke 4:15 states Jesus had been teaching in the synagogues throughout Galilee and had been well received.

The most notable feature of this pericope is that Jesus claims to embody in himself the fulfilment of the Old Testament promise. He is the promised one and his coming and ministry inaugurate the coming of a New Age which is pointed to by the Isaian prophecy.[12] In Luke's scheme of promise and fulfilment, this speech not only sets forth the tone of Jesus' ministry, but that of his disciples in Acts.

One of the strange aspects of the Lukan version of Jesus' rejection at Nazareth is the seemingly unbridged gap between the positive responses of the people in 4:22: "and all spoke well of him (*emartyroun*) and wondered (*ethaumazon*) at the gracious words which proceeded out of his mouth,"[13] and the negative response and rage of vv. 4:28-29. What we have in between is a scene in which Jesus takes the initiative against the people, and by use of the Elijah and Elisha analogy of vv. 25-27 criticizes his own people for their refusal to acknowledge him.[14]

It is the Elijah and Elisha narrative in Luke 4:25-27 that is one of the most important features of this pericope. As L.C. Crockett points out, there are several places in 4:25-27 where Luke departs from the Septuagint.[15] The account in 1 Kings 17 does not say the heavens were closed and the OT gives the length of the famine as three years.[16] Luke also speaks of the famine being "over all the land," instead of in Samaria (1 Kings account). This addition appears to be Luke's contribution and it is parallel to the report of another famine in Acts 11:28. There Agabus the prophet speaks of a "great famine" over all the world. The two are linked together as the former is prophetic of the latter. By making both famines cover a significant geographical area Luke can set the stage for actions which are essential in his scheme of promise and fulfilment.[17]

The famines serve to bring disparate peoples together. In the first famine Elijah, an Israelite, brought relief to a Gentile woman. The second famine was the occasion of the Gentile Church in Antioch (Acts 11:29) sending relief to the brethren in Judaea (Acts 11:28) via Saul and Barnabas. Luke seems to be conscious of the Jewish-Gentile dimension of these famine events as he recorded them. Furthermore, as Acts 11:28 points out, the famine was predicted by a Spirit-inspired prophet; therefore, the whole event (famine and relief) is according to the plan of God, and one anticipated in scripture.

Luke 4:26 then is an allusion to a prophetic text which Luke sees fulfilled in the post-resurrection period. Acts 10-11, the Cornelius Story, can also be related to Luke 4:26. In the Elijah story, Elijah is sent to the Gentile woman, clearly to keep her from starving. According to 1 Kings 17, the widow woman feeds Elijah—hence, an implication of table fellowship. In the Acts 10-11 story of Peter and Cornelius, Peter is commanded to eat what the Gentiles eat, i.e., have table fellowship with them. The fact of Jews and Gentiles living and eating together and supporting one another is a focal point of Luke's communication that God's intention in the New Age is to save both Jews and Gentiles and bring them into a productive mutual relationship.[18]

In the same way we can relate Luke 4:27, the Elisha and Naaman story, to Acts 10-11. Both Naaman and Cornelius are Gentile commanders, and both are cleansed and made clean. In addition to Acts 10-11, Luke 7:1-10 (healing of the centurion's slave) is modeled on the Elisha-Naaman story. Both the centurion and Naaman are devout Gentiles who take the initiative. For Luke, God is free to reveal himself among the Gentiles. Both Cornelius and the centurion are people praised by the Jewish people (Luke 7:5; Acts 10:22).

Taking all these passages together, a pattern emerges which is typically Lukan: the narratives of Elijah and the widow and Elisha and Naaman are used as Old Testament prophecies. Luke 4:25-27 is an announcement of the fulfilment of these prophecies misunderstood by the people, and hence rejected by the people. Luke 4:25-27,then, is a prolepsis not only of the Gentile mission (and certainly not of God's rejection of Israel), but also of Jewish-Gentile reconciliation. It is a prolepsis of the cleansing of the Gentiles so that it is possible for both Jews and Gentiles to live together in the New Age.[19] Luke's use of the LXX was dominated by Jewish-Gentile relations, and his attempt to resolve the problem strives toward the view that in spite of the rejection at Nazareth, the destiny of both Jews and Gentiles is bound up with Jesus Christ and part of God's intention to save and heal both together through Jesus.[20]

The rejection of Jesus at this point does not stop his mission. He escapes the wrath of the people, passing through them and continuing on his way. Actually the rejection sets in motion the whole geographical development which is so important in Luke-Acts. Luke uses the word *eporeueto* (he went away) in 4:30. He uses this word often to indicate wandering from place to place. Jesus, as he goes from place to place, sets an example for the wandering apostles in the Book of Acts. Luke deliberately draws a parallel between Jesus and his disciples.[21] The Nazareth pericope is the beginning of Jesus' "way" which will be climaxed by his death in Jerusalem, but continued in the work of his disciples. The way will eventually lead from Jerusalem to Antioch, Asia Minor and finally Rome. In a certain sense, Luke has put together, on one hand, a fulfilment story ending on a note of success and on the other hand, a rejection story. There is conflict, but the conflict keeps the story moving. The conflict involves the universality of salvation—a mingling of Jews and Gentiles as people to be saved.

Patterned Pericopes of Confrontation and Rejection in Luke-Acts

Luke 4:16-30 contains confrontation, rejection, and an expansion movement in spite of rejection. Luke-Acts in general contains these features along with parallelism. The parallelism lends not only order but presents Jesus as a model for his followers, especially Peter and Paul. It gives continuity between what has occurred and is now happening and then projects order and continuity into the future.

Rejection and confrontation serve as foils against which God's promises are revealed and fulfilled. Even rejection is predicted and thus part of revelation and fulfilment (Acts 3:18, 13:27). Rejection of Peter and Paul by some Jews does not lead to the exclusion of Jews from the people of God. Rejection leads to more preaching—preaching to both Jews and to Gentiles and conversion of both. Even when Paul announces "we turn to the Gentiles" (Acts 13:46; 18:6; 28:28), he continues to preach to and convert Jews (Acts 14:1; 18:8; 28:30-31).[22] In the six patterned pericopes (Luke 4:16-30; 20:9-19; Acts 3:1-4:31; 5:12-42; 13:13-52; 18:1-18) there is an acceptance of Jesus or his disciple followed by a rejection of the same by some of the Jews, often the leaders. Each pericope ends with an ongoing movement either of Jesus' mission in Luke or of the early Christian movement as in Acts. In addition, the pericopes themselves are linked to one another in a variety of ways as we will now note.

1. There is parallelism between the two gospel pericopes inasmuch as they stand at the beginning of the Galilean and Jerusalem ministries respectively. Thus, Luke 4:16-30 was placed at the beginning of the Galilean ministry and quotes Isaiah to set out Jesus' mission to heal, exorcise, preach the good news and forgive sins. Luke 20:9-19 is at the beginning of

the Jerusalem ministry. It is at this point that Luke no longer mentions Pharisees as among those leaders who oppose Jesus. Luke downplays the fact that those considered most orthodox of Jews would oppose Jesus and his offer of salvation. There is also a verbal link between these two pericopes: 4:29 "and they rose up and put him out of the city" (*kai anastanes exebalon auton exō*), and 20:15 "and they cast him out" (*kai ekbalontes auton exō*).

2. Luke 20:17b and Acts 4:11 quote the same Psalm verse (Ps 118:22) i.e., "The very stone which the builders rejected has become the head of the corner" (20:17b) and "This is the very stone which was rejected by you builders, but which has become the head of the corner" (4:11). This literary link is not only between these two individual pericopes but it also provides a connection between the sections *before* Jesus' passion and death and *after* his passion and death.

3. There are several literary links between Acts 3:1-4:31 and 5:12-42. Acts 4:18 ("so they called them and charged them not to speak or teach at all in the name of Jesus") and 5:40 ("and when they had called in the apostles, they beat them and charged them not to speak in the name of Jesus and let them go") are linked by the theme of "speaking in the name of Jesus." Other linking examples are 4:19 and 5:29 (obeying God rather than humans) and 3:13-15 and 5:30-32 (forgiveness and salvation still offered to Israel—a key notion). The literary links in these passages are not surprising since both these passages take place in the context of the missionary effort in the areas of Galilee and Jerusalem, and are separated by an episode dealing with internal problems of the early church. These two pericopes also represent the first persecutions experienced by the early Christian community. In addition to these links, 5:13-52 reads as a shorter version of 3:1-4:31.

4. Acts 5:31: "God exalted him at his right hand as Leader and Savior to give repentance to Israel and forgiveness of sins" is linked to 13:38: "that through this man forgiveness of sins is proclaimed by you and by him everyone ... is freed from everything from which you could not be freed by the law of Moses." This literary link is important as it shows a relationship between a patterned pericope from *before* Stephen's death to one *after* it.

5. Acts 13:13-52 and 18:1-18 are similar because in each of these pericopes Paul explicitly speaks of going or turning to the Gentiles due to the rejection suffered at the hands of the Jewish leaders, Acts 13:46 and 18:6. (Two different Greek verbs are used, but the sense of the sentence is the same). In addition, Acts 13:51: "but they shook off the dust from their feet against them" is linked with 18:6a: "and when they opposed and reviled him, he shook out his garments."[23]

Thus the pericopes are linked rhetorically one to another in its own section (i.e., involving Jesus, Peter, Paul) and to the section following it.

There is also continuity of subject matter. In the texts studied there is emphasis on Jews and Gentiles being saved together as long as there is acceptance of the offer of salvation. Luke 4:16-30 by its Elijah and Elisha analogies points out one of Luke's purposes, i.e., to show God's intention to the New Age is to save both Jews and Gentiles and they are saved together by a productive mutual relationship.[24]

In the allegory of the wicked tenants, Jesus suggests in Luke 20:16 that the vineyard be given to others. This is met with opposition on the part of the people (unlike Mark's version) who express their opposition by "God forbid" (*mē genoito*). Jesus' addition to Ps 118:22-23: "Everyone who falls on that stone will be broken to pieces; but when it falls on anyone it will crush him" (Luke 20:18) suggests only those who reject or oppose the cornerstone will be crushed. Jews are among the saved people—those Jews who accept Jesus.

In Acts 3:1-4:31, Luke continues this theme. As in the two previous pericopes, the key part of the text is in the second action (in this pericope that would be Peter's speech: 3:13-26). This speech does not reject the Jewish people even though they killed the author of life (3:15); the Jews still have priority among God's people (3:26). As long as they repent and accept, they will be offered salvation. In fact only those who do not listen to the prophet like Moses will "be destroyed from the people" (3:23).

Luke continues this narrative by relating the arrest of Peter and John by the temple authorities. The people had been receptive. Luke's division is between those who believe and accept Jesus and those who do not. It is not between Jews and

Gentiles. When Peter addresses the temple authorities who arrested him, he quotes Ps 118:22 as Jesus did in the allegory of the tenants. But Peter says: "This is the stone which was rejected by *you* builders, but which has become the head of the corner" (4:11). In 4:12 Peter interprets the quotation from the Psalm by saying: "And there is salvation in no one else, for these is no other name under heaven given among people by which we must be saved."

Thus, Luke again points out that salvation is not denied to the Jewish people who repent and believe.

Acts 5:12-42 as a summary story similar to Acts 3:1-4:31 also emphasizes Jesus as Savior for all. In fact, here Luke emphasizes salvation of Israel: "God exalted him at his right hand as Leader and Savior to give repentance to Israel and forgiveness of sins" (5:31).

Acts 13:13-52 continues and elaborates on the theme of salvation for both Jews and Gentiles. Paul, in his speech, speaks of Jesus as the promised Savior through whom forgiveness of sins is proclaimed. There is a clear emphasis on both Jewish and Gentile believers even though some Jews stirred up persecution (13:50). Following this pericope in 14:1-2, Paul preached at Iconium converting both Jews and Greeks. This is followed by the statement that *unbelieving* Jews stirred up Gentiles.

Here again, Luke's division of people is between those who believe and those who do not. This is in line with his theme of universalism. The gospel depicts Jesus reaching out to all who will accept him, especially those considered unworthy by devout Jews. In Acts, the word of God is offered to Jews first and then to both Jews and Gentiles who are willing to accept. Christianity as a religion accepts both Jews and Gentiles. The first Christians continued to go to the synagogue as Acts points out time and time again. Paul preaches in synagogues as a regular practice on his missionary journeys.

Finally, Acts 18:1-18 points out, as do the other texts studied, that not all Jews reject the message of salvation. In the second action, Paul goes to a house next to the synagogue and converts the ruler of the synagogue and his household along with many Corinthians (18:8). Jews and Gentiles are brought together; they are saved alongside each other. There is no wholesale rejection of the Jews. In Luke's version of the story of the early church, the restored people of God consists of those who believe in and accept Jesus.

Summary and Conclusion

We have found that the six texts studied not only have a common pattern, but also exhibit similarities which both link successive texts and texts from one section to the other. This was achieved by noting a common significant setting or place within the gospel, similar phrases, quotations of the same psalm, or by noting the same phrase such as "I turn to the Gentiles." In other words, there is similarity in rhetoric. Furthermore, in each there is similar subject matter, i.e., salvation is offered to all people. Jews and Gentiles are saved together. There is no "wholesale" rejection of Jewish people either by Jesus or by his disciples Peter and Paul. Hence, there is continuity between Judaism and Christianity according to Luke. The continuity is assured through the believing Jews and the believing Gentiles who become incorporated into the people of God.

The study, then, of a rhetorical structure helps in the understanding of the theology of a text. It has important implications for the methodology of form and redaction criticism. The multiple interrelationships of texts in a gospel or in a two-volume work such as Luke-Acts indicate that the historical critic must look beyond the individual pericope to the text as a whole. Indeed, an analysis of any text requires that it be looked at within the context of the entire work. For example, in Luke 20:9-19, Luke inserts "God forbid" as a response to Jesus' saying that the vineyard will be given to others (20:16). Luke quotes Ps 118:22 only and adds "Everyone who falls on that stone will be broken to pieces, but when it falls on anyone it will crush him" (Luke 20:18; Mark quotes Ps 118:22-23). When considering this pericope (Luke 20:9-19) and comparing it with Mark for redactional activity, it is reasonable to say Luke as well as Mark wishes to show Jesus rejecting the Jewish people. By his additions, Luke lessens the harshness of Mark's version of the allegory. But if this pericope is considered in conjunction with Acts 4:11, where the same psalm is quoted, and in conjunction with the whole text (Luke 20:9-19), we see there is not rejection of the Jewish people, but rather the statement that Jesus is the means of salvation, the "cornerstone of salvation." Non-acceptance of this cornerstone, or "falling" on that stone is a metaphor for not accepting Jesus. Herein lies the rejection by God—not accepting Jesus.

5

Luke-Acts as an Imitation and Emulation of the Elijah-Elisha Narrative

Thomas L. Brodie, O.P.

One of the basic puzzles in the study of Luke-Acts concerns the very nature of the document. How is it to be classified? As history? Biography? A novel? An historical novel? A cult legend?[1] In recent years particular attention has been given to the view—put forward especially by Charles Talbert, and in a more limited form by Judith Wentling and David Barr—that the genre or type of Luke-Acts is that of a Greco-Roman biography.[2] But, as the cautious work of Wentling and Barr indicates, the matter is still quite undecided.[3]

In a proposal that is complementary to that of Talbert and of Wentling and Barr, it has also been indicated by Raymond Brown (in 1971) and by Martin Hengel (in 1979), that, however much the evangelists drew inspiration from various Greco-Roman literary models, they were particularly indebted to the biblical histories, especially to the narratives which concern such prophetic figures as Elijah and Elisha.[4]

The purpose of this essay is to take that general proposal and to apply it to a specific case—Luke's use of the Elijah-Elisha narrative. What is being put forward here is that, of all the models and sources used by Luke—and he seems to have used many, old and new—the most foundational was the main body of the Elijah-Elisha story (1 Kings 17:1—2 Kings 8:15, a text which is approximately the same length as Mark's Gospel). This was the component around which all the other components would be adapted and assembled.

That Luke should use this prophetic biography is understandable. The story of Elijah and Elisha was not some curious tale, fragmented and faded. It was vivid and alive. Few people

* Notes for Chapter 5 can be found on pp. 172-74

have gripped the Jewish imagination as did the figure of Elijah.[5] He helped the widow, raised the dead, withstood corrupt powers, walked with God, and was taken up into glory. He was a prophet who turned prophecy into action. In many ways he is a hero among heroes, the "prototype of the hero-archetype."[6] Even when he had gone, he lived on in Elisha, and it was said, particularly by the prophet Malachi (2:23), that he would come back. In fact, among the early disciples of Jesus, one of the problems that arose in discussing Jesus' identity was precisely whether he should be regarded in some way as another form of Elijah.[7]

The actual narrative (1 Kings 17:1—2 Kings 8:15) is centered on the taking up of Elijah, and it is thus divided into two parts of about seven chapters each. Whatever may have been the origin of the various episodes in these fourteen chapters,[8] as the text now stands there is, in some episodes at least, a rough balance between the two parts. This is most obvious in the incidents involving women who are in some way impoverished and threatened (1 Kings 17; 2 Kings 4:1-37; 8:1-6). In these texts the story of Elisha is a variation on the story of Elijah.[9]

Apart from the balance between the women-related incidents, both parts of the narrative deal with the following: the miraculous supplying of food and drink (1 Kings 19:1-8 [cf. chap 17]; 2 Kings 4:38-44); Aramean wars (1 Kings 20; 2 Kings 6-7); and the death of a major king (Ahab, 1 Kings 22:1-38; Ben-hadad, 2 Kings 8:7-15). Around the center of the entire narrative is a knot of three chapters (2 Kings 1-3) held together by the repetition (2 Kings 1:1 and 3:5) of the notice of Ahab's death and Moab's rebellion.[10] The precise nature and full extent of the balance between the two parts of the narrative has yet to be researched.

The likelihood that Luke used some ancient text, such as the Elijah-Elisha narrative, is greatly increased by the fact that among authors who wrote in the Hellenistic mold—and Luke was such an author—this type of a procedure was standard practice. The name given this procedure was imitation (Greek, *mimēsis*; Latin *imitatio*) and it sought to rework and reproduce both the form and content of the model or source text in a variety of ways. But it was not slavish. It sought, almost constantly, to surpass the source text—so much so that the idea of imitation became virtually synonymous with emulation or rivalry (Greek, *zēlos;* Latin *emulatio*).[11]

There are four kinds of indications that Luke did in fact use 1 Kings 17:1—2 Kings 8:15 as a basic model.

1. The Inaugural Speech

Inaugural speeches are generally regarded as giving an indication of what a person is about, of what line or model they intend to follow. In Luke's portrayal of Jesus there is such a speech—the programmatic Nazareth speech which is usually seen as encapsulating Luke's entire work (cf. Luke 4:16-30).[12] It begins with a quotation from the prophet Isaiah, and it then goes on, in its final and climactic section, to highlight the example of Elijah and Elisha (4:25-27). The implication, seen clearly by the audience, is that for Jesus these two prophets are to be guiding models.

The fact that Luke should put these two prophets at the climactic point of Jesus' inaugural speech means that they are not just two characters among many. They have a leading role. If Luke regarded them as foundational models for understanding Jesus and his mission, then it is not surprising that in his narrative about Jesus he should give a foundational role to the narrative of Elijah and Elisha. Nothing could be more appropriate.

2. The Presence of the Imitation-Emulation Dynamic

Among those texts which implicitly connect Jesus with the Elijah-Elisha narrative, Jesus is sometimes shown as being quite like Elijah, and at other times as being very different. In 9:51, for instance, "Elijah's 'being taken up' [2 Kings 2:1, 18] is . . . reflected in Luke's use of *analēmpsis* for Jesus,"[13] but just a few verses later, in 9:54-55, Jesus' refusal to call down fire from heaven is a direct antithesis to the OT picture of Elijah (cf. 2 Kings 1:9-14). Thus, in just one brief passage, Luke seems to deal very differently with central episodes from two successive chapters of the Elijah-Elisha narrative. And to some extent such tension runs through other texts which link Jesus with the figure of Elijah. At times, Jesus appears to be Elijah *redivivus*, and on other occasions that identification seems to be rejected.[14] Such a close but tense relationship with an ancient tradition or figure may seem puzzling, and may perhaps be explained by historical conjecture,[15] but in the context of the literary practice of *imitatio* and *emulatio* it is quite understandable. As an accomplished writer, Luke would not describe Jesus in a way that simply *imitated* the OT account of Elijah and Elisha. He would also show Jesus as emulating the OT, as going beyond it. Thus, not only does Luke in his programmatic Nazareth speech give a certain priority to the stories of Elijah and Elisha, but in the subsequent text his narrative appears at times to engage the OT story in a way which accords with the practice of imitation and emulation.

3. *Systematic Literary Use of Specific Texts*

There are at least five texts in Luke-Acts which involve a meticulous reworking of an entire passage from the Elijah-Elisha story.[16] First, the raising of the widow's son at Nain (Luke 7:11-17), however, much it reflects Christian theology, is based, in its narrative development, on a line-by-line adaptation of how Elijah raised the son of a widow (1 Kings 17:17-24).

Second, the episode concerning Jesus and two contrasting characters, the self-sufficient Pharisee and the distraught repentant woman (Luke 7:36-50), turns out to be a Christian dramatization of Elisha's encounter with two women, one of whom, the Shunammitess, displayed contrasting characteristics of self-sufficiency and anguished receptiveness (2 Kings 4:1-37). In this case, the reworking of the OT text consists not so much of a line-by-line adaptation, as of a complex compressing and conflating of the various parts of the older narrative.

Third, the departure of Jesus for Jerusalem (9:51-56) involves a compressing of the OT account of Elijah's departure from the Jordan (2 Kings 1:1-2:6). Fourth, the account of the condemning of Stephen (Acts 6:9-14; 7:58a) involves an adaptation of the condemnation of Naboth (1 Kings 21:8-13). Here,

too, as in the account of raising the widow's son, there is a
precise line-by-line adaptation of the OT narrative, plus a
blending of that narrative framework with later Christian elements. Finally, the stories of Simon the magician and of the
Ethiopian eunuch (Acts 8:9-40) are modeled largely but not
exclusively on the OT stories of Gehazi and Naaman the leper
(2 Kings 5). The account of how Gehazi tried to exchange
God's gift for money has been used to describe how Simon
tried to exchange money for God's gift. And the account of
how the prestigious foreign leper came to Israel and was
renewed through washing (verb *baptizō*) has been used to describe how the prestigious foreign eunuch was baptized.

What emerges from the presence of imitation in these texts
(Luke 7:11-17; 7:36-50; 9:51-56; Acts 6:9-14 and 7:58a; 8:9-40)
is that there are two general areas of Luke-Acts—chapters 7-9
of the gospel, and chapters 6-8 of Acts—where systematic
dependence on the Elijah-Elisha story is an important factor.
This does not mean that dependence is limited to the five texts
mentioned. A more thorough investigation indicates that it
involves at least Luke 7:1-8:3; 9:51-10:20; and certain areas of
Acts 5-9.[17] But it calls attention to those two sections of Luke-
Acts where the dependence is uppermost. Above all it brings
to the fore the fact that the dependence in question is literary
and direct. This is a case of an author before whom the text
lies open. Each of the five cases is so complex and coherent
that it is the theory of direct literary dependence, and that
alone, which can account for the data.

4. The Basic Organization

Finally, there is the similarity between the basic organization
of the narratives. As indicated earlier, the Elijah-Elisha narrative consists of two balanced parts. The same is true of
Luke-Acts. While the Third Gospel presents Jesus, among
other things, as a great prophet, Acts tells of the words and
deeds of Jesus' disciples, and it does so in such a way that those
words and deeds consist sometimes of variations on the example of Jesus.[18] In other words, not only are both narratives
(Elijah-Elisha; Luke-Acts) composed of two parts, but, in both

narratives, the two parts, in some elements at least, balance one another.

Furthermore, in both cases the crucial turning point between the two parts is essentially the same: the taking up to heaven of the master, and the granting of the spirit/Spirit to his disciple(s) (2 Kings 1:1-18; Luke 24:49-53; Acts 1-2). It has, of course, often been noticed that there are similarities between the taking up of Elijah and the ascension of Jesus, but these similarities have sometimes been attributed to oral tradition,[19] or to common dependence on a general form of ascension stories,[20] and so the possibility of sophisticated literary dependence and adaptation has not been adequately explored.[21] It is useful, therefore, to look more closely at the texts:

2 Kings 2:11	Luke 24:51	Acts 1:9-10
1 And it came to pass that they were going along walking and talking,	And it came to pass as he was blessing them,	And as he was saying these things and they were looking on,
2 and behold a chariot of fire and horses of fire separated (*diesteilan*) the two of them,	he was parted (*diestē*) from them,	he was lifted up and a cloud took him out of their sight.
3 and Elijah was taken up in a whirlwind as it were to heaven.	and he was carried up to heaven.	And as they were looking up to heaven as he was going, behold two men stood by them in white garments and said, "Men of Galilee, why do you stand looking to heaven?"

The main purpose of this outline is to show that in each of the texts there are three basic moments: 1. the time of togetherness and communication, 2. the abrupt separation, and 3. the disappearance into heaven. The differences between the texts are considerable but they may be accounted for through deliberate adaptation on Luke's part. On the one hand, he has omitted the stupendous elements (the fiery chariot and whirlwind)—a procedure which is in line with the generally humble and human tone of his writing, and with the picture of Jesus, in contrast to Elijah, as refusing to call down fire from heaven (Luke 9:54-55; cf. 2 Kings 1:9-14). On the other hand, he has made some elaborations to suit the new Christian context and his own particular theological tendencies. Thus, the image of blessing, for instance (Luke 24:51), is part of a larger Lukan emphasis on blessing (cf. esp. Luke 24:30, 50, 53). And the image of the two men in white garments (Acts 1:10) reflects the Christian imagery used to express the events surrounding the resurrection (cf. Luke 24:4; Mark 16:5; Matt 28:2-3). What emerges, therefore, is that just as Luke used the skeleton of the Naboth story as a basis for constructing part of the story of Stephen,[22] so he has used the skeleton of Elijah's assumption as a basis for describing the taking up of Jesus. This is corroborated by the fact that both assumptions are linked with various forms of promising and granting the spirit/Spirit (2 Kings 2:9-10, 15-16; Luke 24:49; Acts 1:2, 8; 2:1-41). But again, of course, Luke's idea of the Spirit is colored and elaborated by Christian experience and reflection.[23]

The essential point, however, is not so much the dependence of the Lukan assumption accounts on that of Elijah, as that this dependence occurs precisely at the mid-point of both two-part works. This is important because dependence at the point which divides the narratives indicates that the (two-part) division of one narrative is connected to the (two-part) division of the other. Luke would hardly build the most basic organizaing factor of his two-part plan, the mid-point, on the most basic organizing factor of the OT two-part text, unless the two plans themselves were connected, unless he had drawn some inspiration from the OT idea of balancing or complementary narratives bridged by an assumption into heaven.

Conclusion

That there is occasional direct literary dependence of Luke-Acts on the Elijah-Elisha story is certain—it is shown by the five specific cases of such dependence. What also seems true—and here lies the specific contribution of this article—is that there is direct dependence on the Elijah-Elisha story for Luke-Acts' overall plan. Such dependence is first suggested by the place given to Elijah and Elisha in the programmatic Nazareth speech, but the decisive indication comes from the fact that, like the balanced Elijah-Elisha text, the balanced two-part narrative is centered on an assumption which, in many ways, appears to be an adaption of the assumption of Elijah.

While there are indeed, in classical antiquity, many references to assumptions or ascents to heaven and many two-part works, there is no two-part work on which Luke shows such occasional direct dependence. Nor is there any two-part work which is divided by an assumption and which could be regarded as a direct literary basis for Luke's account. Hence while it may be true, as Talbert suggests,[24] that the organization of Luke's work into two parts conforms, in some degree, to the organization of various Greco-Roman biographies, it does not seem to be from these biographies that Luke drew his basic plan or model. Such dependence on Greco-Roman models, if it is present, is best seen as a complement to a more basic dependence—that on a narrative from the Bible.

6

A Literary Analysis of the Origin and Purpose of Luke's Account of the Mockery of Jesus

Marion L. Soards

Remarkable differences between portions of the Lukan passion narrative and similar portions of what appears to have been *a* major source for the writing of Luke's Gospel, namely the Gospel according to Mark,[1] cause scholars to draw a variety of conclusions regarding the composition of Luke's passion account. Some critics understand the differences to be the result of Luke's own free composition.[2] Others argue that Luke included disparate traditions, oral and written, into the framework of the Markan passion narrative.[3] Still other scholars contend Luke had a single, integrated, special source, a more extensive version of the passion story. This source formed the basis of the Lukan passion narrative, and Luke redacted Markan material into this other narrative.[4] Only careful study of Luke's passion account allows one to decide responsibly between the options for interpretation.

A fresh study of the Lukan passion narrative might ask, "How is one to imagine that Luke got his information, especially his 'additional' material?" This question will be posed primarily in relation to the *thought* and *content* of the Lukan passion narrative. This study will focus on word statistics and stylistic matters only in a secondary fashion. There are at least two reasons for this approach. First, language and style are weak criteria because of the questionable results they can produce when employed as primary methods.[5] Second, in the present state of biblical studies those doing strictly statistical and stylistic criticism have argued one another into a stalemate.[6] Moreover, in dealing with a complex piece of ancient

* Notes for Chapter 6 can be found on pp. 174-77

literature like the Gospel according to Luke, it is surely a mistake to focus narrowly on the *words* that comprise the larger narrative. Rather than merely analyze words, one should think in relation to the *ideas* that make up the story. The study proposed here will move from two cautious presuppositions. First, the text of the Gospel according to Luke is to be attributed to the hand of the author until demonstrated otherwise. Second, in composing his gospel, Luke used the Gospel according to Mark as *a* major source for his work. From these two presuppositions, this study attempts to analyze a portion of the Lukan passion narrative in order to describe the author's compositional and redactional technique, focusing on one particularly enigmatic part of Luke's general account of Peter's denials, the mockery and examination of Jesus, namely Luke 22:63-65. This scene portrays Jesus being mocked, and it is an important example of the differences between Mark and Luke in terms of the narrative order and details of their passion stories. This study will ask about the origin and purpose of these verses of Luke's Gospel.

To insure clarity in the ensuing discussion a translation of Luke 22:63-65 is provided in which letters of the alphabet mark subdivisions of the verses.

Luke 22:63-65
> 63a And the men who were in charge of him [Jesus]
>   mocked him:
>   b beating him
> 64a and blindfolding him,
>   b they asked him saying,
>   c "Prophesy!
>   d who is the one who hit you?"
> 65 And they said many other things, reviling him.

Narrative Order

Before considering specific differences between Mark and Luke it is helpful to summarize the overall differences in the order of Peter's denials, the mockery, and the Jewish interrogation of Jesus in Mark 14:53-72 and Luke 22:54-71.

Mark	*Luke*
Trial (14:53-64)	Denials (22:54-62)
Mockery (14:65)	Mockery (22:63-65)
Denials (14:66-72)	Examination (33:66-71).[7]

It is readily apparent that the narrative orders of Mark and Luke are completely different. In terms of the mockery, in Mark it occurs at the end of the trial by the council and before Peter's denials; whereas, in Luke it transpires after Peter's denials and before Jesus is examined by the council.

Details

Because of the different positions of the mockery scenes in Mark and Luke, one cannot simply view these as matching accounts.[8] Nevertheless, one may compare the two accounts of Jesus' being mocked as follows:

Where the mockery took place:
  Mark = in the council
  Luke = (apparently) in the courtyard
Who mocked Jesus?
  Mark = some (of the council members [?])
  Luke = the men who were in charge of him
What the mockers did:
  Mark = spat on him, covered his face, struck him, and said
  Luke = mocked him (by) beating him, and blindfolding him, and saying
The demand they made:
  Mark = "Prophesy!"
  Luke = "Prophesy! who is the one who hit you?"
The conclusion to the incident:
  Mark = and the attendants slapped him around
  Luke = and they said many other things, reviling him.

This comparison shows parts of the stories told by Mark and Luke are different, but, these differences exist amidst striking similarities. If Luke had not thought the similarities were more important that the differences he could have narrated another mocking scene exactly like Mark's in the context of the council meeting.[9] Thus, it seems safe to conclude that Luke himself probably regarded these stories as parallels.

Nevertheless, while vv. 63a-64c narrate an event similar to that related in Mark 14:65, noticeable differences exist between the way the mocking is portrayed. Moreover, one must recognize that whole lines in Luke's account (64d and 65) are not matched in Mark's story and should be designated as Lukan material without a Markan parallel. Indeed, one finds an exact verbal parallel to the unmatched material (unmatched in Mark) in Luke 22:64d at Matt 26:68 in the question the mockers pose to Jesus, "Who is the one who hit you?" (*tis estin ho paisas se*). Mark's story has nothing even comparable.

From these observations scholars often argue that the differences here between Luke (22:63-65) and Mark (14:65) are so great as to require that Luke followed another source.[10] But, it is possible, even preferable, to interpret the evidence in a completely different fashion.

The Origin of Luke 22:63-65

The analysis of this scene will begin with 64d. How may one account for the agreement between Luke and Matthew 26:68? The differences between the basic narratives of Luke and Matthew are striking. Except for this line, which is not found in Mark's story, Matthew closely follows Mark's order and action; but Luke differs from Mark's story in both narrative order and detail. The differences between Luke and Matthew make it unlikely that independently they used a common written source. It is even more unlikely that independently Luke and Matthew composed and added exactly the same five-word question (*tis estin ho paisas se*) to the account of the mockery of Jesus. Thus, one best understands this striking agreement by inferring that Luke and Matthew knew the same non-Markan tradition;[11] and, the dissimilarities between the accounts of Luke and Matthew make it unlikely this tradition was written. Therefore, it seems justified to conclude that Luke and Matthew had access to the same oral tradition in Greek.[12] One may infer that in retelling the incident of Jesus' mockery, after the challenge to Jesus to prophesy was narrated, early Christians made clear *what* Jesus was dared to say. Luke and Matthew had heard this clarification of the command to prophesy and independently added *tis estin ho paisas se* to their versions of the story.[13]

Support for this understanding of the agreement between Luke and Matthew exists in other portions of Luke 22. For example: at 22:3 Luke has an agreement with John 13:2, 27 (especially v. 27) concerning Satan's involvement in Judas' betrayal. This agreement is best accounted for by understanding that Luke and John independently employed a traditional early Christian explanation (oral?) of how one of Jesus' disciples could have been moved to betray him.[14]

At four other places Luke and Matthew include similar *ideas or matching phrases* in their passion accounts that they did not draw from Mark—see Luke 22:42 and Matt 26:39, 42—both use the vocative *patēr* and a similar phrase about God's will; Luke 22:48 and Matt 26:50—both have Jesus confront Judas; Luke 22:51 and Matt 26:52-54 (also John 18:11)—both (all three) recount that Jesus rebuked his disciples; Luke 22:62 and Matt 26:75—both alter Mark's *kai epibalōn eklaien* to read *kai exelthōn exō eklausen pikrōs*. In each instance the differences between the general pericopes in which these comparable ideas and matching words occur are greater than the similarities and suggest the use of oral tradition along with Mark's account.[15]

It is possible that what the evangelist knew from oral tradition the other knew from a written source. Since Matthew is closer to Mark here than is Luke, it would seem at first reasonable to say that it is possible that what Matthew (26:68) knew from oral tradition, Luke (22:64d) knew from a written source. There are good reasons, however, to reject this line of reasoning. First, the introduction of a hypothetical written source adds still another stage to the process of reconstruction. The interpretation given above is a simpler reconstruction. Second, if we are to understand that Luke exercised significant editorial freedom in using Mark's story, is it not equally likely he would have done likewise with "another" source? In this case the likelihood of agreement between Luke and Matthew would be less than if we understand them to depend upon a common level of oral tradition. Thus, this line of reasoning brings us to an important observation. Since Luke and Matthew include the same non-Markan tradition[16] in their versions of Jesus' mockery, one may conclude that they were narrating the same event. The implication of this conclusion is that *22:63-65 is Luke's redacted version of Mark 14:65.*

Working from these inferences, one may understand 63a-65 in the following manner: verse 64d ("'who is the one who hit you?'") comes from oral tradition. The unmatched material in 65 ("and they said many other things, reviling him") is Luke's general redactional summary of what Mark tells explicitly in 14:55-61a.[17] Other instances of this type of editorial summarizing are found throughout Luke, e.g., 3:18 and 21:37-38.[18] Verses 63a-64c are Luke's thorough redaction of Mark 14:65.[19] Luke transposed the mockery of Jesus out of the context of the assembly meeting and appropriately altered the description of the group doing the mocking. Mark's account distinguishes "certain ones" who spat on Jesus, slapped him, and challenged him to prophesy from "the guards" who received Jesus with blows after the mockery. But, Luke says that prior to the assembly meeting "the men who were in charge of" Jesus mocked him. Luke seems to indicate the same group here that came out to the Mount of Olives to arrest Jesus, members of the crowd of "chief priest, officers of the temple, and elders" (52b). And so, Luke portrays the same group mocking Jesus *before* the assembly meeting that Mark depicts as mocking Jesus *during* the assembly meeting.[20]

The alteration in order brings the sequence of Luke's narrative into compliance with the order delineated in the first passion prediction at Luke 9:22 ("'The Son of man must suffer many things, and be rejected by the elders and chief priests and scribes, and be killed, and on the third day be raised'"). The differences between Luke and Mark achieve at least three results: (1) Jesus' courage is accentuated by having Peter's cowardice precede.[21] (2) Deep irony is inherent in Luke's narrative when Peter remembers that Jesus had prophesied his denials, and then, the men holding Jesus imply he is no prophet with their mocking game.[22] (3) After Peter's denials and the treatment that Jesus suffers, the readers might expect him to be easy prey for the assembly.[23]

The Purpose of Luke 22:63-65

Above all, Luke's arrangement of the scenes reinforces the

image of Jesus' determination. When Jesus stands before the assembly (66a-71c) he has already witnessed Peter's denying him three times (54a-62b), and he has already suffered the indignity of injurious, mocking treatment from his captors (63a-65). Despite being abandoned and abused, Jesus is not intimidated as he faces the assembly. Rather, he displays the equanimity that comes from knowing that his destiny is the realization of the will of God (42a-d). Throughout 22:39-71 — in prayer, at his arrest, during Peter's denials, while he is mocked, and in his appearance before the assembly—Jesus is absolutely *steadfast*. He acts in his customary fashion and thereby assures that the plan of God will come to proper realization.

Moreover, one understands that Jesus acts in full control of his destiny and, thereby, fulfils God's plan by means of the *irony* that Luke developed in this portion of the passion account.[24] Luke built into his narrative an unstated communication between himself and his readers. He created a two-story phenomenon wherein there exists a sharp contrast between appearance and reality. The readers are invited to participate with Luke in the higher level of the narrative. Such participation provides a covert corrective to a false understanding of the story based merely on appearance. This claim must be illustrated.

In appearance, Jesus is the victim of those "in charge of him" as he waits to go before the assembly (63a-65). This group plays a cruel game. They blindfold Jesus, take turns hitting him, and as they strike him, they dare him to reveal exactly who delivered the blow. The implication of their taunt is that Jesus is incapable of prophesying.

The readers of this story enjoy a privileged position. If they take their cues from Luke, they move to the higher level of the narrative from which they gain a new perspective on the events of the passion. From this vantage point, it is possible to know what the members of the group have yet to discover, i.e., *Jesus is a prophet*. In the episode that precedes the mockery, Peter denied Jesus three times, fulfilling exactly the prophecy of Jesus. Luke arranged the scenes of the passion in 22:54-71 so that the readers have information that allows them to contrast Jesus' implied inability to prophesy with his true power as a prophet. They see that Jesus is no mere victim; indeed, he is the true prophet who sees and does God's will. Those "in charge" of Jesus are ignorant and their false assumption about Jesus' prophetic impotence causes them to suffer the brunt of their crude joke. The effect of Luke's narrative technique is that the apparent victim becomes *the one in charge* and the apparent authorities becomes the victims of their own ignorance. It would be only the unsympathetic, disengaged, or dim-witted reader who would not perceive the implications of Luke's carefully managed plot.

A Final Note

Examination of the story of Jesus' mockery in Luke 22:63-65 supports neither the contention that Luke's Gospel is based on a proto-Luke nor the claim that Luke took recourse to a written, coherent special passion narrative source that was itself an independent account of the passion of Jesus. In fact, the results of this study suggest it is artificial to think about Luke's composition of the passion narrative only in terms of written sources. It seems clear that at points Luke drew on oral material in producing his own account of the mockery of Jesus. This finding suggests that the early Christian community continued to tell of Jesus' last days after that story was committed to writing. Indeed, a well-known and much discussed quotation of Papias by Eusebius confirms this interpretation, "For I did not suppose that information from books would help me so much as the word of a living and surviving voice" (Hist. Eccl. 3:39:4). This statement is testimony of tradition among early Christians. Perhaps it is not only artificial but even misleading to think of *an* oral or *a* written passion account, for Luke could have known a dozen or more passion narratives—oral and written. Thus, only through open-minded analysis of each pericope of the Lukan passion narrative can one finally describe how Luke formed his story and why.

Recurrent Narration as a Lukan Literary Convention in Acts: Paul's Jerusalem Speech in Acts 22:1-21

Marie-Eloise Rosenblatt, R.S.M.

1. Introduction

PAUL'S SPEECH IN JERUSALEM AS FOCUS

Paul's Jerusalem speech provides a particularly rich text as a basis for exploring some of Luke's theological concerns in Acts.[1] These concerns are reflected in the composition of this speech and emerge when Luke's composition of Paul's apology[2] is refracted through the lens of the literary method Gerard Genette outlines in *Narrative Discourse: An Essay in Method.* This study directs its attention to Acts 22 in light of Genette's categories of order of event, speed of narration, and repeated narration of a single event. Included in this analysis will be a brief reference to other texts in Acts which illustrate use of the literary convention of recurrent narration. Finally, a reflection will be offered on the effects of applying this method to the interpretation of Acts 22.

Like Luke, Genette takes very seriously the encapsulation of event within time, and this may be identified as the starting place for applying Genette's method: the sequence of events within Acts understood as comprising a temporal construct unto themselves, a unified narrative world created by an author.[3] This author is conscious of beginning a story, including major events, intentionally excluding some, creatively modifying others, and shifting the focus from one character to another. He frequently places the telling of portions of the story on the lips of chosen characters yet reserves other

---

* Notes for Chapter 7 can be found on pp. 177-78

moments of the narration to himself, and he ends the story purposefully.

In analyzing plot sequence, Genette identifies chronological cues within the narrative that indicate conventional or transposed order of event, retrospective and anticipatory breaks in the chronological order, and the long or short duration the report of an event takes in the narrative, i.e., whether the event seems to be speeded up or slowed down in its telling by the author.

Mood in Genette's scheme includes the literary convention of shifting point of view in which events are told through the eyes of a variety of spokespersons who differ in their relative degree of knowledge or understanding of the events they narrate.[4] A number of events can be reported by a variety of different designated narrators or speakers within a story, or the same event can be reported by a variety of speakers in what is called multiple or recurring narration.

It is this particular literary phenomenon, a single event retold or renarrated several times by a variety of speakers, which is illustrated by the several tellings of Paul's Damascus experience (9:1-19; 22:6-16; 26:12-18). A discussion of Luke's preoccupation with the Damascus event in Paul's spiritual history is, however, recontextualized by recognizing Luke's use of repetitive narrative in a number of other events in Acts as well: the multiple reporting of the Peter-Cornelius encounter (Acts 10:1-11:18), the council of Jerusalem (Acts 15:1-29; 21:25), and Paul's appearance before Festus in Caesarea (25:6-12, 14-21, 24-27; 26:32; 28:17-19). While the review of Paul's Damascus experience in Acts 22 is usually placed in a frame which includes Acts 9 and 26, with a comparison and contrast made among the trilogy of texts, Genette's literary methodology re-frames the question about the reasons for Luke's repetition of the story about Paul's vision of Jesus.

2. Temporal Order in the Jerusalem Speech

RETROSPECTIVE AND ANTICIPATORY REFERENCES

By order Genette identifies the sequence of events in a narrative told in chronological order.[5] Paul's speech as a whole represents a break in the narrative flow of Acts, for the content of the speech is an interruption or anachrony in the chronological order of Acts. Its content refers to events in the more remote than recent past. As such, the speech in its entirety is narrative analepsis, flashback or retrospection, a return to a temporal point which the narrative flow of Acts has already bypassed. It takes the hearer back to a point previous to this moment in the story, to the beginning of Paul's life. Paul's birth and upbringing in Jerusalem were never mentioned earlier in Acts.

Presumably, the "young man" (Acts 7:58) outside the walls of Jerusalem is the one "brought up in this city" (Acts 22:3). The time of Paul's education in Jerusalem reported in Acts 22:3, then, refers to a time earlier than Acts 7:58, even though it comes much later in the text. One may ask why Luke chooses this later point in the narrative to refer to the early history of Paul. It seems an intentional break in order. For Jesus and John the Baptist, the only other persons for whom Luke includes "early life" narratives, the recounting of infancy and childhood is located early in the story, at a chronological point before the narration of their ministries. In the case of Paul, the chronological and narrative order are disrupted, and details about Paul's early life and upbringing emerge much later in the narrative, after the missionary journeys have been reported.

The retrospective order is also broken by anticipations that leap ahead to events "beyond" the narrative moment or beyond the narrative frame of the speech. The prophecy of Jesus to Saul, "Rise, and go into Damascus, and there you will be told all that is appointed for you to do" (22:10), is fulfilled later in the same episode, when Paul arrives in Damascus (22:11) and receives a commission from Ananias (22:14-15).[6] The fulfilment is another prophecy itself of Ananias to Paul, "for you will be a witness for him to all people of what you have seen and heard" (22:15), anticipates the missionary activity of Paul that extends beyond the narrative content of the speech. Jesus' warning to Paul, "They will not accept your testimony about me" (22:18), anticipates the situation Paul finds himself in "later," at the time of giving this speech, when he is rejected in Jerusalem.

As anticipatory breaks in the chronological order, both the words of Ananias and Jesus have thus already been fulfilled in the narrative. After Paul's conversion, his preaching in Jerusalem to the Hellenists was rejected, and because of danger to his life, Paul's friends spirited him away to Tarsus (9:28-30). The commission of Ananias has been fulfilled in the previous narration of Paul's missionary activity, and is being fulfilled in this very speech, when Paul recounts what he has seen and heard.

TEMPORAL ORDER OF EVENTS IN PAUL'S SPEECH

While the content of the entire speech is a retrospective or flash-back, there are breaks in the consistency of the "past-ness." The past is not told in order, from remotest past to most recent past. Considering Acts 22:1-21 as the chronological reference point, and comparing the order with the overall narrative of Acts, the order from remotest to most recent past would be a) Tarsus birth, b) upbringing in Jerusalem, c) involvement in Stephen's death, d) persecution of the followers of the Way, e) mandate to carry out arrests in Damascus, f) conversion on road to Damascus, g) encounter with Ananias, h) return to Jerusalem and vision of Jesus, i) mandate to preach to the Gentiles, j) departure on missionary journeys, k) return to Jerusalem and attack by the mob.

A closer look at the sequence of events within the speech reveals the reshaping of temporality by Luke, a reshaping which calls attention to an association of the witness Paul with the witness Stephen. The order of events in the defense speech is: a, b, d, e, f, g, h, *c*, i, j, k. Thus, the event out of order is the reference to Paul's involvement in Stephen's death. The narrative, already a retrospective, is interrupted by another anachrony or break in chronology. It may be argued that the theme of Paul's speech has now become his mandate to preach to the Gentiles. At this point the speech is interrupted (22:21-22), calling attention to this missionary directive. Nevertheless, the event transposed out of chronological order also is being highlighted: the Stephen-Paul connection.[7] The event of Stephen's death (22:20) is still present to Paul as memory and reflection, and it re-emerges at this narrative moment as retrospective of an event earlier in Paul's life (7:58-8:1), a memory which expresses what is happening in the present—Paul's rejection—and perhaps also anticipation of the fate awaiting Paul himself.

OTHER ANACHRONIES AND TEMPORAL INTERRUPTIONS

Other interruptions of conventional chronological order include two "time warps" recorded in the narration. The first is the address of Jesus to the persecutor: "Saul, Saul" (22:7) which echoes that period earlier in the narrative when Paul was called Saul.[8] No reason is ever given in the narrative of Acts for the change of name to Paul, only an editorial aside that he was known by both names (13:9). But "Saul" is, from the perspective of this methodological analysis, a temporal assignation of identity which reverts the speech-giver's "time" to a moment earlier in the narrative. "Saul" signifies an identity that was once bound up with the Jerusalem temple establishment (7:58; 8:1-3; 9:1-2) on one hand, and the burgeoning church establishment in Damascus (9:22), in Jerusalem (9:26-28) and Antioch (11:25-26; 13:1-3) on the other.

A second anachrony is indicated by the appellation "I am Jesus of Nazareth" (22:8), which is the name of Jesus according to his geographical earthly place of origin, the name by which he was known before he was proclaimed Messiah. Paul insists at various points that he preaches the resurrection of the Lord and of the Messiah—this is why he is on trial and persecuted (23:6; 24:15; 25:19; 26:23). Indeed, Paul addresses the speaker as *kyrie* (22:8, 10). But here in the conversion event, the name "Jesus of Nazareth" associates the heavenly speaker with a terrestrial city and suggests a season before the resurrection, certainly earlier than the events narrated in Acts.[9] Jesus of Nazareth has been named in third person previously in Acts (e.g., Acts 2:22; 3:6; 4:10), references made in the context of sermons which reviewed doctrine about Jesus.[10] This is the only time Jesus names himself as "Jesus of Nazareth," a technique which thrusts the reference again back into the narrative which precedes Acts, the story of Jesus in Luke's Gospel (Lk 4:16). Thus, the appellation creates a chronological rupture in the narrative of the conversion, and is a kind of invasion of the remote past into the more recent past represented by Paul's recounting of his confrontation with Jesus.

ACCELERATION AND DECELERATION OF PACE

Observations about Luke's control of speed can be made at three junctures or transitions in the Jerusalem speech. In the first, the transition from the road to Damascus to Damascus itself is summarized by a statement that Paul was led into the city because he was blinded by the light (22:11). This accelerates the narrative to the next moment of the meeting with Ananias. The acceleration is emphasized and the narrational speed increased by the omission of the transitional material that would have explained how Ananias and Saul met with each other, an encounter reported in the first narration of the conversion (9:10-17). The narrative in 22:12 simply jumps to this meeting, with its healing and baptism of Saul. The words of Ananias in the first account emphasized why he had been sent to Saul—to help him recover his sight (9:17). In this second account, the oration of Ananias is prophetic mandate and commissioning of Saul.[11] In the first account, the healing from blindness was followed immediately by baptism (9:18). In this second account, between the healing from blindness (22:13) and the baptism (22:16) is interposed the prophetic instruction. Thus, the rhythm of the narration of 22:11-16 is quickened on one hand by the omission of detail and lengthened on the other hand by the interpolation of an oracular instruction.

A second transition involves a summary statement, implying a passage of time between the baptism and the vision in the temple. A spatial change from Damascus to Jerusalem is indicated by a participial construction: "when I had returned to Jerusalem" (*hypostrepsanti eis Jerousalēm*, 22:17). There are no indications about the length of the interval between Paul's conversion and the vision in the temple. It can be surmised that it was at "several days" (*hēmeras tines*, 9:19) and "many days" from the lengthier narration earlier in Acts (*hēmerai hikanai*, 9:23). As a consequence of this gap, the speed of the narration of 22:16-17 is accelerated by the omission of post-conversion details about Paul's preaching activities in Damas-

cus. The Acts 22 account omits the material from the first
narration in Acts 9 that of Paul's mixed reception by his
hearers and the consequent life-endangering opposition that
rose up against him in Jerusalem before he was hastily re-
directed down to Caesarea and on to Tarsus by his supporters
(9:19-30). Again, such omission speeds the pace of the Jerusalem speech.

A third instance of transition involves Paul's vision of Jesus
in the temple (22:17-21).[12] The disclosure of the vision is a
narrative leap backward to an indeterminate occasion when
Paul made a visit to Jerusalem. The situation described earlier
in the narrative (9:19-30) is omitted from the recounting of the
temple vision in which Jesus warns Paul to leave the city. The
effect is to dramatize, accelerate, and intensify the narrative by
focusing on a spiritual experience of short duration, Paul's
conversation with Jesus. The conversation is brief, and its
narration has verisimilitude with an actual encounter. The
command, "Get quickly out " (22:18), could locate the vision
at some moment in his brief Jerusalem preaching tour, after it
was clear that his debates with Greek-speaking Jews (*Hel-
lēnistēs*, 9:29) were only generating hostility and attempts to
kill him. In the earlier narrative, it is the supporters of Saul
who hear of the plots and come to his rescue (9:30). In the
account Paul gives in 22:17-21, it is the warning given directly
by Jesus that constitutes the command to leave Jerusalem.
The repetition of Jesus' command in his revelation to Paul to
leave and go to the Gentiles (22:21) marks the end of Paul's
speech; the crowd breaks into an uproar, and Paul cannot
continue his appeal.

The vision is highlighted for three reasons then: its function
in marking the end of Paul's dramatic speech, its brief but
pointed duration which accelerates the narration of the entire
speech, and its singulative character (it is reported only once in
Acts).

REJOINING THE NARRATIVE GAPS

The narrative is "seamed" or joined by the very eruption of
this hostility from the Jerusalem audience. Paul's rehearsal of
being driven from Jerusalem earlier in his life is linked with a

re-enactment of the hostility on the occasion of his speech. From this perspective, the retrospective has "rejoined" or caught up with the main narrative. The rejoining is accomplished by a fusion of past experience of hostile rejection with present experience of hostile rejection.

The speech is actually concentrated on three dramatic scenes: the conversation with Jesus on the road to Damascus (22:7-11), the oracular instruction of Ananias (22:14-16), and the conversation with Jesus in the temple vision at Jerusalem (22:17-21). These three internal scenes in the speech, which themselves each lasted but a short time, absorb the telling time of the address itself. As focal scenes, they slow the narrative pace in comparison with summaries which pass over a great distance of time quickly. But the three scenes themselves also move quickly, with information pared to a minimum. Events of brief duration, rather than long duration, monopolize the narrative, forcing attention on these experiences rather than on the events of longer duration which are summarized, implied or omitted.

The contrast with an earlier version of Paul's conversion in chapter 9 indicates which events Luke is highlighting at this point in the narrative of Acts: Paul's two visionary experiences of Jesus, and the oracular instruction by Ananias about Paul's mission. Several aspects of the speech represent recurring narration, but this narrational convention highlights by contrast the singulatively-told episode of Paul's vision in the temple. Another reason the temple vision draws attention to itself is its chronological dislocation, or relocation to a point earlier in the story of Acts than Paul's delivery of his Jerusalem speech.

FIRST PERSON NARRATION AND IMMEDIACY

The defense speech of Paul is an example of mimetic narration. Luke's presence as a narrator is here translated into the presence of one of the characters of Acts, Paul. Luke assumes the persona of Paul and the "I" which projects the desperate appeal is still Luke, but narrating events through the voice of Paul. One effect of this dramatic model is to eliminate the distance between author and story, speaker and event, between narrator and narration. But the immediacy of Paul to the events of his own life, communicated by a first-person narration, stands in contrast to the immediacy the hearers can have to these same events.[13] The scenes and dialogues immediate to Paul in memory consist of events which his hearers in the Jerusalem audience did not share. They are events lying at either temporal or geographic distance from his hearers. What is "near" geographically because of the connection with Jerusalem—the connection of Paul's upbringing, early association with the religious establishment, the vision in the temple—is remote temporally in relation to his audience. What is distant geographically—birth in Tarsus, the experience on the road to Damascus, the encounter with Ananias, a Jewish Christian of Damascus—is also remote temporally.

What critically reinforces the remoteness, however, is neither temporal nor geographic distance, but hostility between Paul and his audience. The hostility is not overcome, in spite of Paul's effort to identify himself with his audience on the basis of their shared dedication to Jewish tradition (22:3). This distance or hostility is all the more dramatic because of the contrasting nearness to events or "sympathy" of casting Paul as speaker in first person, narrating the formative spiritual experiences he has had, and the analogous "nearness" of the narrator Luke, who has stepped into the character of Paul in order to be less distant, as an observer or third-person narrator would be. The highly controlled mimetic narration reproduces an aspect of Paul's life which contrasts with the earlier narrative in Acts 9, when he was the agent of persecution. Now the "conversion" has become defined as a situational change in status, in which he himself has become the target of persecution and violence.

RECURRING OR MULTIPLE NARRATION AND SHIFTING POINT OF VIEW

The Jerusalem speech, a narrational variant since it is first-person narration in contrast to the third-person account of Paul's life in Acts 9, has a number of parallels in Acts. Like other biblical writers, Luke quite commonly employs this convention of re-narration to reproduce the telling of events in the form of speeches, sermons, dramatic dialogues, and letters.

Various reasons for the re-narration can be proposed, but for the moment it is useful to be reminded of the pervasiveness of the phenomenon of multiple narration as a literary convention in Acts.

If all examples of re-narration of Paul's conversion experience are counted, then there are four retellings (9:1-19, 27; 22:1-16; 26:1-23), including the one given by Barnabas when he introduces Paul to the community in Jerusalem and assuages their doubts (9:27). Besides the Damascus vision itself, other elements of Paul's speech are re-narrated in Acts, such as Paul's involvement in the death of Stephen (7:58; 8:1; 22:20), his characterization as a persecutor (8:1-3; 9:1-3, 13-14, 21; 22:4-5, 19; 26:9-11), and the oracular appearance of Ananias and his instruction of Paul (9:10-17; 22:1-16).

The conflict between Paul and the Jewish crowd in the temple precincts which involves Paul's arrest is an event that illustrates a multiplication of narrative perspectives through shifting point of view. A variety of relations are illustrated among designated speakers and receivers within the narrative. The episode is first presented to readers in third-person observer narration, with both narrated and reproduced speech (21:27-36). It is included in the second person as part of a letter Lysias sends to Felix, with Lysias acting as the "I" narrator (23:26-30). It is part of the accusation Tertullus brings against Paul in Caesarea before Felix (24:6), part of the first-person narration of Paul, who recounts the arrest in his defense before Felix (24:11-19), and also part of the defense Paul makes before Agrippa and Festus (26:21).

Repetitive narration can also be identified in the legal hearing before Festus in Caesarea after he has just assumed the office of governor, during which Paul appeals to have his case heard in Rome. The hearing is presented first in third-person observer narration with both narrated and reproduced speech (25:6-12). Then the hearing is reported by Festus to Agrippa in a one-to-one conversation in which Festus is the "I" narrator of the events (25:14-21). Then it is reported again by Festus addressing Agrippa and the group assembled in the audience hall (25:24-27), reviewed by Agrippa himself in speaking about Paul to Festus (26:32), and finally placed on Paul's own lips in speaking to Jews in Rome (28:17-19). The change of speakers also accomplishes a change in perspective, for the event assumes a different meaning when viewed through the eyes of one character rather than another.

3. Conclusion

Signs of Luke's hand as an artist can be identified by his use of a number of literary conventions, available to the literary critic at the surface level of the text of Acts. Of particular focus in this study is the conventional use of multiple or recurring narration as it affects the interpretation of Paul's Jerusalem speech in Acts 22:1-21. However, the analysis of this speech is re-contextualized when Paul's Damascus experience is seen as one example among several other episodes in Acts which Luke chooses to retell in a number of ways. Further investigation could be made about those events in Acts targeted by Luke as subjects to be re-narrated. Along with Paul's Damascus vision, for example, are circumstances connected with the conversion of Cornelius, the council of Jerusalem, Paul's arrest in Jerusalem, and his hearing before Festus in Caesarea.[14]

One notes that by shifting the point of view and rounding out the narrational perspective, Luke creates the illusion that the story is present, not distant. The reader is brought closer to some events, the ones which absorb and preoccupy the text's telling space.

The shifting point of view in each case is a gradual turning over of the meaning of an event. As a narrative pondering, it is an exercise in reflection, for it slows the narration by requiring the forward movement to be shifted backwards. The dialectic of going forward by backtracking and retelling the events builds up as a narrative hologram. Thus, these re-told events are "stilled," and given various narrative frames and a variety of contexts. In one frame, Luke the narrator addresses the reader as an objective observer and teller. In another, a principal character, such as Paul, speaks to an audience he feels alienated from, before whom he is on the defensive. In a third frame, characters who are agents or participants, but not carriers of the main action, can be described as witnesses of the events in the conversation they have with one another, or the letters that are sent. These instrumental characters in the story also serve as narrators. Their reports in the official, public forum show the gradual advance of the mission of Paul from private experience, to church policy, to public encounter with the government in the juridical forum.

This methodological approach has additional bearing on the interpretation of Acts 22, for it becomes appropriate when analyzing the accounts of Paul's vision to give attention to the moment in the narrative when the vision is retold, by what narrator the experience is recounted, and to whom the vision is retold. One immediate effect of this method is to note that the retelling of Paul's Damascus experience occurs at widely separated chronological moments in Acts, in contrast to the relatively compressed periods of narrative time in which retellings of the other events are accomplished.

This farflung retelling results in the Damascus experience acquiring a longer "run" on the stage of Acts than other events. Its replay marks that moment when the persecuted church began to spread to territories beyond Jerusalem, when it began to regroup its forces and Paul's work as an evangelist formally commissioned by the Jerusalem elders began. It punctuates the end of his active and freely-chosen circuit of the Mediterranean and communities of Asia Minor, and the end of the formal interrogations reported in Acts. As such it sets up three temporal poles. The first in Acts 9 and second in Acts 22 circumscribe the period of Paul's active mission and the third in 26 frame Paul's testimony as a prisoner subject to interrogation and trial.

One might say that the story of the church's life unfolding in Acts—its founding, its spread and its time of trial—finally becomes enshrined and summarized in the retelling of Paul's life. Luke's multiple narration of Paul's life-story, as well as its dramatization at certain points within the overall narrative of Acts, seems essentially related to Luke's message about the significance of the apostle's individual life as interpretation, prototype, and carrier of the life of the community.

PART III

Theological and Thematic Essays

8

Following Jesus:
Discipleship in Luke-Acts[1]

Dennis M. Sweetland

Discipleship, according to Luke, characteristically takes the form of a journey. To be a disciple of Jesus one has to follow him along the way that he walks from Galilee to Jerusalem and ultimately to God. After a general introduction to the journey theme in Luke-Acts we will examine the call and commissioning stories in the gospel. In this way, the main themes of discipleship in Luke-Acts will be introduced. The remainder of our study will consist of an expanded discussion of these motifs.

1. The Journey Theme

Luke did not invent the journey motif; he found it in his Markan source and expanded upon it.[2] Luke is following Mark's lead when he uses "to follow" (*akoloutheō*) as a figurative expression for discipleship (Luke 5:11; 9:49, 57, 61; 18:28). When Jesus says to individuals "follow me" (5:27; 9:59; 18:22; cf. 9:23), he is inviting them to become personally attached to him as he journeys toward his goal.[3] In Acts, the risen Lord maintains this close relationship with his disciples when he pours out the Holy Spirit upon those who repent and are baptized (Acts 2:33, 38). It is the "Spirit of Jesus" (16:7) that serves as the bond of union between Jesus and his disciples[4] and empowers them to function as his representatives as they bring the message of the salvation of God to the end of the earth. Luke pictures Jesus as a traveler with a definite purpose. At the beginning of his ministry Jesus says, "I must preach the

---

good news of the kingdom of God to the other cities also; for I was sent for this purpose" (Luke 4:43). At the outset of the travel narrative (9:51-19:44), Luke informs the reader that Jesus has firmly resolved to go to Jerusalem, where his ascension will occur (9:51). Throughout the remainder of the travel narrative, Luke indicates numerous times that Jesus and his disciples are continuing their journey to Jerusalem.[5]

The travel motif also permeates Luke's story of the early church in Acts. The risen Jesus provides the outline for Luke's second volume in 1:8 when he says, "You shall receive power when the Holy Spirit has come upon you; and you shall be my witnesses in Jerusalem and in all Judea and Samaria and to the end of the earth." After the descent of the Holy Spirit at Pentecost (Acts 2:1ff.) and the "witnessing" in Jerusalem (chapters 2-7), the missionary efforts of the early church spread to Judaea and Samaria (chapters 8-12) and, eventually (chapters 13-28), to Rome.[6] Whether the missionaries are named, as are Philip (8:5, 26), Peter (10:19ff.), and Paul (chapters 13-28), or not named (8:4; 11:19ff.), one realizes that their travels are not aimless wanderings but rather are watched over and guided by God (14:27; 16:6-10).[7]

One can continue to speak of discipleship as a journey, even after Christian communities are formed, because the ultimate goal of Jesus' journey is God, not Jerusalem. Luke's use of "to follow" in a figurative sense indicates that the journey motif was never meant to be understood merely in physical terms. He portrays Christian discipleship "as the identification of oneself with the master's way of life and destiny in an intimate, personal following of him."[8] There is a connection, therefore, between the journey motif and the life of faith. Luke suggests that following Jesus on the journey to God means making progress in the life of faith (cf. Luke 8:15; 17:5-6).[9] The journeys of Jesus and his followers in Luke-Acts indicate that the third evangelist wants his readers to understand the life of faith as active, not static.

2. Call and Commissioning Stories

THE CALL OF THE FIRST DISCIPLES (5:1-11)

According to Luke, Jesus calls and commissions his first

disciples while in a boat on Lake Gennesaret (Luke 5:1-11). By transposing and editing his source (Mark 1:16-20; cf. John 21:1-19), Luke emphasizes several themes that he will develop throughout the gospel and Acts.

(1) Individuals are presented as following Jesus only after they have heard his words and observed his powerful deeds. Because the authority of Jesus' word has already been established (cf. Luke 4:32, 36), Luke is able to present Peter as lowering his nets simply in response to Jesus' "word" (5:5). Before Peter, James, and John follow him (cf. Mark 1:21-34) Jesus performs exorcisms and healings in Capernaum (Luke 4:31-37) and heals Peter's mother-in-law (4:38-39). Luke realizes that powerful deeds such as these are ambiguous (11:14-19) and can be performed by non-Christians (Acts 8:9-11), but on many occasions in the gospel (Luke 5:17-26; 7:18-23; 8:2; 19:37-38) and in Acts (9:35, 42; 13:12; 16:25-34; 19:17) he emphasizes that miracles can be a catalyst for faith.[10]

(2) Jesus associates with sinners and other outcasts. When Luke records Peter's comment, "Depart from me, for I am a sinful man, O Lord" (Luke 5:8), he is pointing to Jesus' association with social outcasts and sinners, by means of which he offers them forgiveness and reconciliation (cf. 18:9). Although this behavior would have shocked many first-century Jews (cf. 5:30), Luke understands it to be a necessary part of the divine plan. The salvation of God is to be offered to all, especially sinners (cf. 5:32).

(3) The call to discipleship includes a missionary responsibility. Jesus refers to Peter's future missionary activity when he says to Peter, "henceforth you will be catching men" (Luke 5:10). This theme is connected closely to the witness motif when Jesus says to his apostles: "you shall be my witnesses in Jerusalem and in all Judea and Samaria and to the end of the earth" (Acts 1:8). Giving witness to the risen Christ,[11] like the missionary responsibility, is an important component of discipleship in Luke-Acts. Neither task is restricted to Peter.

(4) Christian discipleship can be described as "following" Jesus. Luke's first use of *akoloutheō*, which implies "an internal attachment and commitment to Jesus and the cause that he preaches,"[12] occurs in this call story (Luke 5:11).

(5) The one who chooses to follow Jesus must adopt a

radical stance toward possessions. When Luke tells us that Peter, James and John "left everything" in order to follow Jesus (Luke 5:11), he is intensifying the teaching about possessions that he found in his source (cf. Mark 1:16-20). Luke stresses this point elsewhere in the gospel (5:28; 14:33; 18:22, 28; 21:3-4) and in Acts (2:45; 4:34; 5:1ff.).

THE CALL OF LEVI (5:27-32)

In the two pericopes which precede the call of Levi one learns that Jesus restores social outcasts to community (Luke 5:12-14) and forgives sinners (5:17-26). The present story reinforces this understanding of Jesus and reminds the reader about the kind of individuals who followed Jesus as his disciples. When he says "follow me," Jesus is inviting Levi to form a close personal relationship with him and to join him on the journey (5:27). The Lukan addition, that Levi "left everything" (5:28; cf. Mark 2:14), agrees with the response of the first disciples (Luke 5:11).

After he leaves his tax office, Levi invites many tax collectors and sinners to a great feast at his house (Luke 5:29f.). Some suggest that Levi, by inviting those who need the gospel to his house where the gospel is proclaimed (5:32), is being presented by Luke as engaged in the missionary activity of "catching men" (5:10).[13]

Luke also alters Mark's version of this story when he says that Jesus has come to call sinners "to repentance" (Luke 5:32). With this addition Luke has brought out an element that he sees as integral to the teaching of Jesus. In a general sense, *metanoia* involves a radical conversion from all that is evil and an absolute commitment to God.[14] Luke understands this not as a once-for-all total change, but as a process to be worked out within the Christian community.[15] This call to repentance is found throughout the gospel and Acts.[16]

THE CHOOSING OF THE TWELVE (6:12-16)

Luke tells the reader that Jesus, after praying all night, "called his disciples, and chose from them twelve, whom he named apostles" (Luke 6:12-13). In rewriting Mark's introduction, Luke has introduced the motif of prayer into this story (cf. Mark 3:13-19). Throughout the gospel Luke portrays Jesus as one who prays (Luke 3:21; 5:16; 6:12; 9:18, 28, 29; 11:1; cf. 23:34, 46). Jesus teaches his disciples a prayer (11:2-4), and urges them to pray always and not lose heart (11:5-8; 18:1-8; cf. 22:40). In Acts, the early church is pictured as following Jesus' teaching and example concerning faithfulness in prayer (e.g., Acts 1:14-24; 2:42, 46, 47; 4:24-31; 12:5, 12; 20:36; 21:5).[17] This has led many to conclude that Luke considers prayer to be among the more important elements of discipleship.[18]

THE MISSION OF THE TWELVE (9:1-6)

The power and authority Jesus possesses (cf. Luke 4:32, 36), and has used both to exorcise and to heal, are demonstrated in the four miracles stories (8:22-56) which immediately precede his giving power and authority to the twelve (9:1). Deviating from his source (cf. Mark 6:6-13), Luke informs the reader that Jesus sent out the twelve specifically "to preach the kingdom of God" (9:2). This commission closely associates the twelve with what Jesus has said is his main role (4:43). Luke's unambiguous portrayal of Jesus and the twelve as carrying out the same ministry is scarcely accidental. Once they "are clothed with power from on high" (Luke 24:49; Acts 1:8), enabling them to begin their post-resurrection missionary task, it is the power of Jesus that allows these early Christian missionaries to be successful (e.g., Acts 3:12, 16; 4:7-12) as they preach the kingdom of God (Acts 8:12; 19:8; 20:25; 28:23, 31).

THE TEACHING ABOUT DISCIPLESHIP (9:57-62).

The second pericope (see Luke 5:27; 18:22) in which Jesus explicitly says to an individual "follow me" occurs shortly after the travel narrative has begun (9:57-62). Luke has edited this story in order to emphasize the radical nature of Christian discipleship (cf. Matt 8:19-22). In the first of three exchanges Jesus indicates that anyone who wishes to follow him must be willing to sacrifice security. In the second exchange Jesus issues the invitation "follow me" and instructs this individual, "Go and proclaim the kingdom of God" (Luke 9:60), thus drawing attention to the relationship between the mission of Jesus and that of his disciples (cf. 4:43; 9:2). In the third exchange, Jesus' response, "No one who puts a hand to the plow and looks back is fit for the kingdom of God" (9:62), complements his answer in the previous exchange, "Leave the dead to bury their own dead" (9:60). Thus, accompanying Jesus and assisting him in his missionary task take priority over certain responsibilities one has to one's family, both living and dead.[19]

THE MISSION OF THE SEVENTY (10:1-20)

Luke is the only gospel writer to mention the mission of the seventy. This pericope (Luke 10:1-20) is a Lukan construction, based on material from both Q (see Matt 9:37-38; 10:7-16; 11:21-24; cf. 10:40) and Mark, and is patterned after the sending of the twelve.[20] It is enough to point out here that: (1) These missionaries, like the twelve, are closely associated with the mission of Jesus. They use the power and authority that Jesus gives them (Luke 10:19) in order to exorcise and heal, and, like Jesus and the twelve, they preach the kingdom of God (10:9, 11). This motif is further emphasized when Jesus says, "The one who hears you hears me, and the one who rejects you rejects me, and the one who rejects me rejects the one who sent me" (10:16). (2) The previously mentioned themes of hearing Jesus (10:16, cf. 10:24) repentance (10:13), and prayer (10:2) are all referred to in these verses. (3) Individuals other than the twelve are involved in the missionary enterprise. This foreshadows the situation in Acts when numerous members of the early church will function as missionaries. (4) The Christian disciple should rejoice and be joyful (10:17, 20; cf. 10:21).[21] The atmosphere of joy, wonder, praise, and blessing, that pervades the infancy narrative (e.g., 1:14-28, 46, 58; 2:10) is found throughout the gospel[22] and Acts[23] and should characterize the disciple's attitude toward God's work in human history.

THE RICH RULER (18:18-30)

The call to establish a close relationship with him is issued by Jesus to the rich ruler (Luke 18:22) with the same words he used in 5:27 and 9:59, "follow me." The lack of a positive response from the ruler, when he is invited to "sell all" that he has and follow Jesus (18:22), leads Jesus to add that, without God's help, it is impossible for a rich person to enter the kingdom (18:24-25). A comparison between the rich ruler and Jesus' disciples is invited when, in 18:29, Peter says that he and others have fulfilled the conditions that Jesus presented to the rich ruler. Jesus responds by noting that those who have preferred nothing to the kingdom of God will "receive manifold more in this time, and in the age to come eternal life" (18:30). Although he has substantially altered his source here (cf. Mark 10:30), Luke agrees with Mark that the "more" which one will receive in this life means association with the new family of Jesus, i.e., the church.[24]

Our examination of the numerous invitations to discipleship Jesus extends has given us a general understanding of what Luke believes Christian discipleship entails. The remainder of this study will be dedicated to a closer examination of several of the motifs already mentioned. (1) Hearing the words of Jesus (2) about forgiveness and reconciliation leads the disciple (3) to repent, believe in Jesus, and be baptized (4) into Jesus' new community, (5) which is known for its unselfish use of possessions.

3. Listening/Hearing

In his sermon in the temple area (Acts 3:12ff.) Peter identifies Jesus as the eschatalogical prophet of whom it was said, "You shall listen to him in whatever he tells you" (3:22; cf. Deut 18:18ff.). This agrees with what the voice from heaven says at the transfiguration, "This is my Son, my Chosen; listen to him!" (Luke 9:35). Listening to Jesus is a necessary first step toward discipleship, but it is not enough for one who would be Jesus' follower. In the sermon on the plain, Jesus says that those who hear his words must also incorporate them into their lives (6:46-49). This same theme appears later in the gospel, when Jesus identifies his true family as "those who hear the word of God and do it" (8:21), and when Jesus responds to the woman who praises his mother by pronouncing as blessed "those who hear the word of God and keep it" (11:28).

The listening/hearing motif is even more prominent in Acts than it is in the gospel. Luke has included in his second volume some twenty-eight speeches which account for about thirty percent of the text. As in the gospel, those who hear the word are usually moved to action. In Acts 2, for example, one learns that after hearing the words of Peter and the disciples at Pentecost many respond positively and ask, "What shall we do?" (2:37). Peter answers, "Repent, and be baptized, every one of you in the name of Jesus Christ for the forgiveness of your sins" (2:38). Throughout Acts one sees the disciples functioning as witnesses to what they have seen and heard and large numbers of people coming to believe because they hear the word of God.

Luke also uses the motif of listening/hearing to emphasize the unity between Jesus and his disciples. This is seen clearly in Luke's editorial expansion of a traditional saying found in Mark 9:37 (cf. Matt 10:40; 18:5; Luke 9:48). Only Luke adds to this saying that those who "hear" the Christian missionary "hear" Jesus (Luke 10:16; cf. 9:48).

4. Forgiveness/Reconciliation

Jesus tells those who listen to him that he has come to seek and to save the lost (Luke 19:10; cf. 15:1-32). Early in his public ministry Jesus says to a paralytic, "your sins are forgiven" (Luke 5:20) and announces to the onlookers that "the Son of man has authority on earth to forgive sins" (5:24). In the sermon on the plain he describes God as merciful (6:36) and tells his audience to forgive, and they will be forgiven (6:37; cf. 17:3-4). Jesus also forgives the sins of the woman who anoints his feet (7:48), and teaches his disciples to pray, "Father ... forgive us our sins" (11:2-4; cf. 12:10). As risen Lord he tells the eleven and those with them, "that repentance and forgiveness of sins should be preached in his name to all nations" (24:47).

Luke's interest in "the forgiveness of sins" is also evident in Acts. Peter does what the risen Lord has commanded when he advises his audience at Pentecost to repent and be baptized "in the name of Jesus Christ for the forgiveness of your sins" (Acts 2:38) and when he tells Cornelius that all the prophets bear witness to Jesus Christ so that "everyone who believes in him receives forgiveness of sins through his name" (10:43). Together with the apostles, Peter informs the Jewish council that God exalted Jesus "at his right hand as Leader and Savior, to give repentance to Israel and forgiveness of sins" (5:31). Paul, who is sent to the Gentiles by the risen Lord so that "they may receive forgiveness of sins" (26:18), also proclaims forgiveness of sins in Jesus' name (13:38-39).

When Luke looks back at the Christ-event, one way in which he sums up its effect is by the phrase "the forgiveness of sins."[25] The good news of the kingdom, that Jesus has inaugurated the long awaited era of salvation (cf. Luke 19:9; Acts 4:10-12), includes the message of the forgiveness of sins which is to be preached to all nations (Luke 24:47; Acts 26:15-18).

5. *Repentance, Belief, and Baptism*

REPENTANCE

Peter faithfully carries out the command of the risen Jesus, that "repentance" as well as forgiveness of sins be preached in his name to all nations (Luke 24:47), when he says to the crowd that has listened to his pentecost speech, "Repent, and be baptized every one of you in the name of Jesus Christ for the forgiveness of your sins" (Acts 2:38; cf. 3:19; 8:22). The call to repentance appears first in the preaching of John the Baptist (Luke 3:3, 8; cf. Acts 13:24) and is rooted in the ministry of the earthly Jesus. Jesus announces that he has come to call sinners "to repentance" (Luke 5:32), reminds the crowds that the people of Nineveh "repented at the preaching of Jonah" (11:32), and tells the seventy that Tyre and Sidon "would have repented long ago" if they had witnessed his mighty works (10:13). While Jesus warns that the one who does not repent will perish (13:3, 5; cf. 16:30), he also comforts his audience by

speaking of the joy in heaven over one sinner who does repent
(15:7, 10; cf. 15:22-24, 32).

In Acts, Peter urges his audience at Pentecost (Acts 2:38),
those who hear him later in the temple area (3:19), and Simon
the sorcerer (8:22) to repent. Together with the other apostles
he announces that God has exalted Jesus "at his right hand as
Leader and Savior, to give repentance to Israel" (5:31). Later
in Acts, the reader learns that God has "granted repentance
unto life" to the Gentiles (11:18) as well as to Israel. Luke also
portrays Paul as a missionary who preaches the message of
repentance (17:30; 20:21; 26:20) which leads to baptism (19:4-
5; cf. 13:24).

BELIEF

The positive side of repentance is faith (*pistis*). In a general
sense *pistis* implies obedience, trust, and hope as well as the
acceptance of the "good news."[26] Luke understands this to
include hearing the word of God, holding it fast in an honest
and good heart, and bringing forth fruit with patience (Luke
8:15). Jesus implies that faith leads to salvation when he says
that the devil will come and take away the word from some,
"that they may not believe and be saved" (8:12; cf. 8:50). The
connection between faith and salvation is more explicit when
Jesus says to the woman who anointed his feet, "your faith has
saved you" (7:50) and when Paul says to his jailer, "believe in
the Lord Jesus and you will be saved" (Acts 16:31).

Through his disciples (Acts 8:26-38; 10:44-48; 13:46-48;
14:8-10), the risen Jesus offers repentance, forgiveness of sins,
and sanctification to those who have faith in him (26:17-18).
Many who hear the word of God (4:4; 8:12f.; 11:21; 14:1; 15:7;
18:8) or see the signs and wonders of the apostles (5:14; 9:42)
come to believe. In his sermon to Cornelius, Peter says that
everyone who believes in Jesus "receives forgiveness of sins
through his name" (10:43; cf. 13:39, 48; 16:31). The one who
hears the word of God is expected to believe (15:7; cf. 4:4;
Luke 1:20). In fact, the early Christian community is composed
of those "who believed" (Acts 2:44; 4:32; cf. 15:5).

BAPTISM

In addition to repenting and believing, Luke implies that the Christian disciple must be baptized in Jesus' name. Luke refers to the baptism of John numerous times in his two-volume work and informs the reader that Jesus himself was baptized (Luke 3:21; cf. Acts 1:22). John tells the multitudes that someone mightier than he is coming who "will baptize you with the Holy Spirit and with fire" (Luke 3:16). The necessity of baptism is implied when Peter says "Repent, and be baptized every one of you in the name of Jesus Christ for the forgiveness of your sins; and you shall receive the gift of the Holy Spirit" (Acts 2:38), as well as in the stories about the conversion of the Ethiopian eunuch (8:37-38), Paul (9:18), Cornelius (10:48), and those who believed the preaching of Philip (8:12).

Nowhere, however, does Luke state that baptism is absolutely necessary for salvation. The three thousand pentecost-day converts were baptized (Acts 2:41), but no mention is made that any of the original disciples, including the mother of Jesus, was baptized (1:12-15). Although he states that Apollos, who had been instructed in the way of the Lord and spoke and taught accurately the things concerning Jesus, only knew the baptism of John (18:25), Luke does not report that Apollos ever received Christian baptism.

Various solutions have been suggested concerning the relationship between baptism and Christian discipleship. An important insight is that Luke gives priority to the reception of the Holy Spirit.[27] This helps to explain the emphasis on the Spirit at Pentecost and the note that Apollos was "fervent in spirit" (Acts 18:25), although he only knew the baptism of John. The importance of the Holy Spirit for Luke leads him to suggest that it is possible to receive the Holy Spirit apart from baptism and water (cf. 8:12, 15-17; 9:17-18; 10:44-48). While the necessity of baptism is not stated by Luke, it is clearly implied in several places (cf. 2:38; 8:12, 37-38; 9:18; 10:48).

6. Discipleship and Community

In the gospel, Luke alludes to an organized and communal

way of life for Christians when he says that "those who hear the word of God and do it" are Jesus' mother and brothers (Luke 8:19-21; cf. 18:30), that several women provided for Jesus and his disciples out of their means (8:1-3), and when he portrays the followers of Jesus as gathered together (24:33, 52). The most obvious example of Luke's interest in the communal dimension of discipleship, however, appears in his second volume. In Acts, the disciples of Jesus are said to be of "one accord" as they pray together (Acts 1:14) and to be of "one heart and soul" as they live in common, their generosity insuring that there will be no needy among them (4:32; 2:44-45). Luke understands the community to be organized, although he is somewhat vague about its exact structure. In the gospel there is little distinction among the followers of Jesus as the twelve and the seventy are assigned the same tasks.[28] In Acts, however, one finds a proliferation of roles and functions as the early church solidifies and struggles with troublesome issues. While it is clear that some individuals and groups (e.g., Peter, James, the elders) function in leadership roles, the exact nature of their roles is not always clear.

Luke actually presents the reader with several different models for the church in Acts: (1) the idealized Jerusalem community, (2) the community which is centered around Antioch and its missionary activity, and (3) the community which is reflected in Paul's speech to the Ephesian elders (20:18ff.).[29] It is difficult to decide which, if any, model Luke prefers, because he presents each structure (Jerusalem, Antioch, and Ephesus) in a positive light. Luke presents the reader with a church that is in the process of growing and developing as it is guided through history by the Holy Spirit in accordance with the plan of God. Luke takes for granted that a hierarchy exists within the Christian community. What he is concerned with is the appropriate behavior of those in authority. This leads him to point out quite clearly that church leaders must pattern their behavior after Jesus, who gave himself as servant, and must conduct themselves humbly as servants of all (Luke 22:25-27).

The Christian community, as Luke presents it, is also very much concerned with the celebration of the Eucharist.[30] This motif appears in the multiplication of the loaves (Luke 9:10-

17; cf. Mark 6:41-43), in the Lord's supper (Luke 22:14ff.), and in the Emmaus story (24:30ff.). The same formula—take, bless, break, and give—appears in all three pericopes (9:16; 22:19; 24:30). In Acts, Luke reports that the Eucharist was celebrated for the converts at Troas (Acts 20:7, 11) and indicates that the religious life of the community is centered in the Eucharist (2:42ff.). After the ascension, the community is united through the Lord's supper to the Risen One who is present in the Eucharist.[31]

7. *Possessions*

Luke's concern about the relationship between the Christian disciple and wealth is widely recognized. In the gospel, Luke includes virtually all Markan pericopes devoted to wealth and possessions, all appropriate Q texts, and many other relevant passages not found elsewhere in the New Testament. In Acts, Luke presents several positive examples of almsgiving and describes the early Jerusalem community as sharing wealth and possessions. Luke includes in his gospel the well-known saying of Jesus, "For it is easier for a camel to go through the eye of a needle than for a rich person to enter the kingdom of God" (Luke 18:25). This saying implies that it is virtually impossible for the rich to enter the kingdom of God. In this pericope one also learns of Jesus' demand that this would-be follower leave "everything" and follow him (18:22). This same radical attitude toward possessions is found in the call of the first disciples (5:11) and the call of Levi (5:28). In the sermon on the plain Jesus says: "Blessed are you poor, for yours is the kingdom of God" (6:20), "but woe to you that are rich, for you have received your consolation" (6:24; cf. 12:16ff.; 16:19-31). This reminds one of Mary's comment that God "has put down the mighty from their thrones, and exalted those of low degree; he has filled the hungry with good things, and the rich he has sent empty away" (1:52-53). The story of the widow's mite (21:1-4; Mark 12:41-44) also suggests that the rich face great difficulties in their attempt to enter the kingdom of God.

This harsh attitude is modified slightly in Acts when Luke presents the members of the early church as sharing wealth and possessions. There are hints of this position in the gospel itself, especially in the story of the conversion of the rich tax collector Zacchaeus (Luke 19:1-10),[32] where one learns that salvation of the rich is possible (cf. 18:27). In order to be saved, however, a rich person must receive Jesus joyfully and share Jesus' active concern for the poor and the exploited.

In his second volume, Luke does not suggest that would-be disciples are required to sell all their possessions. The model Luke presents in the early chapters of Acts is one in which possessions are shared with other members of the community (Acts 2:44-45; cf. 4:32). Later, however, Tabitha and Cornelius are commended for their almsgiving (9:36; 10:2, 4, 31).[33]

And still later in Acts, Luke presents Paul, a tentmaker (Acts 18:3) who works to support himself, as a model for the Ephesian elders to follow as he takes care of his own needs and the needs of his companions (20:34; cf. 21:24) and the weaker members of their community (20:35).

The Christian ideal, as Luke presents it, is a community in which there are no needy people (cf. Acts 4:34). But how does one reach this goal? Since none of these practices in Acts is presented as a departure from an original ideal, it is likely that Luke sees each as a transformation or outgrowth of an earlier stage. As the church continues its journey with Jesus, the risen Lord, new models for the correct use of possessions emerge which, though different, are in continuity with the past.

Regardless of the model adopted, one must remember that in Luke's eyes how one handles possessions is an indication, a symbol, of one's interior disposition, whether one is responding positively or negatively to the word of God.[34] Luke does not portray possessions as evil in themselves, nor do they necessarily prevent a positive response to the word of God (cf. Luke 18:28). But Luke is convinced that one must choose between serving God and serving mammon (Luke 16:13). Wealth can be used for good, but in many cases it creates priorities which prohibit the rich from doing the will of God.

8. Summary

Jesus associates with sinners and outcasts in order to offer them forgiveness and reconciliation. In Acts, in accordance with the divine plan and under the guidance of the Holy Spirit, it is Jesus' disciples who bring the message of the salvation of God "to the end of the earth." After hearing Jesus' words and observing/hearing about his powerful deeds, many of these individuals follow Jesus. Included in this proclamation is the message of repentance and the forgiveness of sins, which comes about through belief in the Lord Jesus Christ. It is also implied that the Christian disciple must be baptized in Jesus' name. During this journey with Jesus, what it means to be Jesus' disciple is gradually revealed. One learns that discipleship requires a willingness to sacrifice security and place one's commitment to Jesus and his work ahead of certain familial obligations. Discipleship includes membership in a new family and brings with it a missionary responsibility. The disciple is intimately associated with Jesus, especially when preaching the kingdom of God; for those who hear the Christian missionary, hear Jesus. God's work in human history should bring forth both a prayerful and joyful response from the follower of Jesus.

Luke envisions Christian life as organized and communal and indicates that the Eucharist, rooted in the ministry of Jesus, is an important celebration in the early Christian communities. He does not consider riches evil in themselves, nor does he suggest that they necessarily prohibit one from responding positively to the word of God. In many instances, however, they do prevent their owner from doing the will of God. The disciple must follow Jesus' example and be mercifully and compassionately involved in caring for the poor. The way in which one manages one's possessions is an indication of whether one is responding positively or negatively to the word of God. One must give help to others rather than amass wealth for oneself.

9

God the Father in Luke-Acts

Robert L. Mowery

Although Luke-Acts contains twenty explicit references to God the Father, these references are unevenly divided between these two books. Luke contains seventeen references, with the first reference occurring in the second chapter (2:49) and the last reference occurring in a resurrection narrative (24:49). In contrast, Acts contains only three references to the Father, and all three are in the first two chapters of the book.

We will discuss these references to the Father in four sections.[1] The first two sections will examine the gospel's references to the Father, with the first section discussing the references to the Father of *Jesus* and the second section concentrating on the references to the Father of the *disciples*. The third section will examine the references to the Father in Acts 1-2, while the fourth section will reflect on the significance of the references to the Father in Luke-Acts.

1. God the Father of Jesus in Luke

The Gospel of Luke contains a series of references to God the Father of *Jesus*. We will discuss these references in the order of their occurrence.

The first reference to the Father is in the question of the twelve-year-old Jesus, "Did you not know that I must be in my Father's house?" (2:49). The reference to the Father appears in an ambiguous phrase which, as Fitzmyer notes, could also mean "(involved) in my Father's affairs" or "among those people belonging to my Father."[2] Although the Lukan infancy narrative calls Jesus "Son of the Most High" (1:32) and "Son of God" (1:35), it never refers to God as the Father prior to

---

* Notes for Chapter 9 can be found on pp. 180-81

this verse. The first reference to the Father does not occur until the Lukan Jesus utters his first words.

Luke 9:26 contains the only Lukan Son of Man logion which refers to the Father. Unlike Mark 8:38, which ascribes glory only to the Father, Luke 9:26 speaks of the glory of the Son of Man, the Father, and the holy angels.

Jesus' words in 10:21-22 contain five explicit references to the Father. Although the two references in 10:21 are in Jesus' words addressed *to* the Father, the three references in 10:22 are in his words *about* the Father. In 10:21 Jesus addresses God as "Father, Lord of heaven and earth" and as "Father." In 10:22a Jesus speaks of the Father as "my Father," but in 10:22b and 10:22c he uses the absolute form "the Father." All of these references are references to the Father of Jesus.[3]

All of the gospel's other references to the Father of Jesus occur in the passion and resurrection narratives. In 22:29 Jesus declares to the disciples, "As my Father appointed a kingdom for me, so do I appoint (a kingdom) for you."[4] This logion, which occurs only in Luke, declares that Jesus acted for his disciples in the same manner as the Father acted for him.

In 22:42 Jesus prays, "Father, if thou art willing, remove this cup from me; nevertheless not my will, but thine, be done." The Gospel of Mark also refers to the Father at this point, for it indicates that Jesus prayed the words, "Abba, Father," in Gethsemane (14:36). Luke 22:42 lacks Mark's "Abba" and has a vocative *pater* ("Father") instead of Mark's nominative; however, in agreement with Mark, Luke claims that Jesus not only addressed the Father in prayer at this significant point but also subjected his own will to his Father's will. Jesus' prayer to the Father represents the focal point of this unit.[5]

In 23:34 Jesus prays from the cross, "Father, forgive them; for they know not what they do." This whole logion is textually uncertain.[6] If this logion was a part of the original text of Luke, it provided an additional link between the Father and the Lukan passion narrative.

In 23:46, immediately before his death, Jesus cried, "Father, into thy hands I commit my spirit!" Although this cry repeats the words of Psalm 31:5, its opening word "Father" is a Lukan addition to this citation.[7] Through the words of this psalm,

Jesus expressed his trust and confidence in the Father at the moment of his death. Note that both the first words of the Lukan Jesus (2:49) and the last words of the dying Jesus (23:46) refer to the Father.

In 24:49 the risen Jesus declared to the eleven, "And behold, I send the promise of my Father upon you." This final reference to the Father in Luke occurs in the final words of Jesus in this gospel.

The references to the Father in Luke 22-24 periodically remind the reader of the unique relationship between the Father and the Son. While the Markan passion and resurrection narratives contain only one reference to the Father (14:36), the Lukan passion and resurrection narratives contain a series of references (22:29, 42; 23:34(?); 46; 24:49). All of these references identify the Father as the Father of *Jesus*.

Many of the gospel's references to the Father of Jesus were taken from the evangelist's sources. At least six of the seven references in Luke 1-10 rest on pre-Lukan material. Although the first reference (2:49) is in a logion of uncertain origin,[8] the second reference (9:26) is in a Lukan version of a Markan-logion and the other five references (all in 10:21-22) are in Q material. The five references in Luke 22-24 are in passages of disparate origin:

> 22:29—"my Father" is in a logion which presumably
>   preserves a pre-Lukan tradition;[9]
> 22:42—"Father" was in the pre-Lukan form of this
>   saying, either Mark 14:36 or a non-Markan
>   tradition;[10]
> 23:34—"Father" is in a textually-uncertain logion
>   (whose origin, if authentic, is unclear);
> 23:46—"Father" is a redactional addition to an OT
>   citation;
> 24:49—"my Father" is in a phrase which is probably
>   redactional.[11]

Redactional references to the Father of Jesus apparently occur only in 23:46 and 24:49, perhaps in 2:49, and possibly in 23:34. Note that most of these redactional references are in Luke 22-24.

All of the references to the Father in the Gospel of Luke are in words of Jesus. These dominical logia contain four prominent themes: the claim that God is the Father of Jesus, an emphasis on the appellation "Father" in prayers of Jesus, an emphasis on the sovereignty of the Father, and an emphasis on the authority of the Son.

1. Many of these logia explicitly identify the Father as the Father of Jesus. Jesus directly addressed God as "Father" five times (10:21 [twice]; 22:42; 23:34 [?], 46). and he explicitly referred to God as "my Father" four times (2:49; 10:22; 22:29; 24:49).

2. When Jesus addressed God in prayer in Luke, he usually used the appellation "Father." Unlike Matthew and Mark, Luke never indicates that Jesus addressed God as "God."[12]

3. Many of the "Father"-logia emphasize the sovereignty of the Father. Verse 10:21 praises the Father as the "Lord of heaven and earth"; 10:22 identifies the Father as the one who delivered "all things" to Jesus; 22:29 names the Father as the one who "appointed a kingdom" for Jesus; 22:42 emphasizes the Father's will; 23:46 declares that the dying Jesus committed his spirit into the Father's hands; and 24:49 speaks of "the promise of my Father."

4. Several of these logia also emphasize the authority of the Son. Verses 10:22 and 22:29 indicate that the Father has given authority to the Son; 9:26 declares that the Son of Man will come in glory; and 24:49 portrays the risen Jesus authoritatively speaking of his role in sending the Father's promise.

In addition to these references to the Father, the Gospel of Luke contains twelve references to Jesus as God's Son.[13] These references to the Son naturally imply that God is the Father. All but one of the references to the Son are in Luke 1-10, and all of the references to the Father of Jesus which precede the passion narrative are in these chapters. The Lukan passion and resurrection narratives contain all the other references to the Father of Jesus plus the only other reference to the Son (22:70). The intervening chapters, Luke 11-21, lack references to both the Father of Jesus and the Son.

The references to the Father and the Son in Luke 1-10 establish Jesus' identity as the Son of God and his unique relationship with the Father, while the references in Luke 22-

24 periodically remind the reader of Jesus' identity during the crucial passion and resurrection narratives. The evangelist apparently felt no need to repeat these themes during the intervening chapters, Luke 11-21. These intervening chapters identify the Father in a different way, for they identify the Father as the Father of the *disciples*. This is the theme to which we will now turn.

2. God the Father of the Disciples in Luke

The Gospel of Luke contains five dominical logia which refer to God as the Father of the *disciples*:

> 6:36 "Be merciful, even as your Father is merciful,"
> 11:2 "Father, hallowed be thy name,"
> 11:13 "how much more will the heavenly Father give
> the Holy Spirit to those who ask him?"
> 12:30 "and your Father knows that you need them,"
> 12:32 "Fear not, little flock, for it is your
> Father's good pleasure to give you the
> kingdom."

Three of these logia contain the phrase "your Father" (6:36; 12:30, 32), with the pronoun "your" (*hymōn*) being a plural pronoun. The other two logia are preceded by second person plural verbs (11:2, 13). None of these logia is addressed to a lone individual.

The evangelist indicated that Jesus directed at least four of these logia to the disciples. The introductory words in 11:1-2a claim that Jesus taught the Lord's Prayer—including the address "Father" in 11:2—to his disciples. The resumptive reference in 11:5 indicates that he directed 11:5-13, including the reference to the Father in 11:13, to the same audience. The opening words of 12:22 indicate that he also taught 12:22-40, including the words "your Father" in 12:30 and 12:32, to the disciples. By directing these four logia to the disciples rather than a wider audience, the evangelist defined the references to the Father in these logia as references to the Father of the disciples.

The reference to the Father in 6:36 also seems to be a reference to the Father of the disciples. Although 6:36 stands in a section of the sermon on the plain which is introduced by an ambiguous audience reference (6:27, "But I say to you that hear"),[14] it follows the promise that those who obey the imperatives of 6:35a "will be sons of the Most High" (6:35b). This verse and its promise seem to be addressed to disciples.[15] If the second person plural verbs and pronouns in 6:35 refer to disciples, the second person plural pronoun "your" in the phrase "your Father" in 6:36 presumably also refers to disciples.

Four of these five logia probably rest on Q traditions, and the references to the Father presumably stood in the pre-Lukan forms of these traditions.[16] The fifth logion (12:32), which has no Synoptic parallel, surely also rests on a pre-Lukan tradition. The evangelist apparently did not create any redactional references to the Father of the disciples.

The only theme which is present in all five of these logia is the claim that God is the Father of the disciples. Two of these logia emphasize the Father's grace, for 11:13 declares that the heavenly Father will "give" the Holy Spirit to those who ask him and 12:32 stresses the Father's pleasure to "give" the kingdom to the "little flock." Verse 12:30 focuses on the related theme of God's providence; note that the subsequent verse uses the divine passive when promising that "these things will be added to you" (12:31). Other themes occur in 6:36, which calls the disciples to imitate the merciful Father, and 11:2, which prays that the Father's name be hallowed.

We must also note the portrayal of the father in the parable of the prodigal son (15:11-32). The father in this parable is an earthly father. When the younger son confesses to his father, "I have sinned against heaven and before you" (15:18, 21), he maintains a distinction between "heaven" (i.e., God) and his father. Within the context of Luke 15, however, this human father appears to be a symbol or representative of God the Father. Marshall, for example, claims that "the attitude of the father is meant to depict that of God,"[17] and Fitzmyer comments, "As it now stands in the Lucan Gospel, the parable presents the loving father as a symbol of God himself."[18]

A recurring emphasis in Luke 15 is the sharing of joy over the "finding" of the "lost." In the first parable of this chapter, a shepherd calls together his friends and neighbors to rejoice with him after he found his lost sheep (15:6), and in the second parable a woman calls together her friends and neighbors to rejoice with her after she found her lost coin (15:9). In the parable of the prodigal son, the father implores his elder son to join the celebration after the prodigal returned (15:28, 32). Verse 15:10 declares that "there is joy before the angels of God over one sinner who repents" (cf. 15:7).

3. God the Father in Acts 1-2

Acts contains only three explicit references to the Father, and all three are in the first two chapters of the book. In 1:4 the risen Jesus charged the disciples (in indirect speech) "to wait for the promise of the Father." The phrase "the promise of the Father" is nearly identical with the phrase "the promise of my Father" in Luke 24:49. In 1:7 the risen Jesus told the disciples, "It is not for you to know times or seasons which the Father has fixed by his own authority." These words are reminiscent of Mark 13:32, a logion which also refers to the Father. Having omitted this logion from Luke, the author of Luke-Acts seems to be presenting a version of it in this verse.[19]

The third reference to the Father occurs in Peter's preaching following the outpouring of the Spirit at Pentecost:

> Being therefore exalted at the right hand of God, and having received from the Father the promise of the Holy Spirit, he [= Jesus] has poured out this which you see and hear (2:33).

The "promise" which Jesus received from the Father is "the promise of my/the Father" mentioned in Luke 24:49 and Acts 1:4.

The three references to the Father in Acts 1-2 have various common features. Two of these references occur in the direct or indirect speech of the risen Jesus (1:4, 7), and two of them are in the phrase "the promise of/from the Father" (1:4; 2:33). All three are absolute references to "the Father"; none has a possessive modifier such as "my" or "your."[20]

Acts seldom identifies Jesus as the Son, for such references occur only in 9:20 and 13:33. Acts' reserve concerning this title parallels its reserve concerning the title "Father."

4. God the Father in Luke-Acts

The references to the Father in Luke-Acts represent only a small fraction of the references to God in these two books. The gospel contains at least 250 references to God, including approximately 120 references which use *theos* ("God"), about thirty-five which use *kyrios* ("Lord"),[21] various others which use other divine appellations,[22] and more than seventy which use the divine passive or other circumlocutions of the divine name.[23] The gospel's seventeen references to the Father represent about one-fifteenth of this book's references to God. The three references to the Father in Acts represent an even smaller fraction of the references to God in that book.

Nineteen of the twenty references to the Father in Luke-Acts are in words of Jesus, including the reference in indirect speech in Acts 1:4. The lone exception (2:33) performs the function of certifying that the Father had fulfilled the promise to which the risen Jesus had referred when he spoke of "the promise of my/the Father" (Luke 24:49; Acts 1:4).

Luke-Acts explicitly associates the Father with the passion narrative, the gift of the Spirit, and various other past and future events. Two or three verses declare that Jesus addressed the Father in prayer during the passion narrative (Luke 22:42; 23:34 [?], 46). The first of these verses associates Jesus' impending death with the will of the Father, while 23:46 stresses Jesus' trust and confidence in the Father at the moment of his death. Three other verses (Luke 24:49; Acts 1:4; 2:33) associate the gift of the Spirit with the design and intention of the Father. The references to the Father in Luke 2:49 and 10:21-22 and the references to the Son in Luke 1-10 associate the Father with the period prior to the passion, while the logion in Acts 1:7 affirms the Father's authority over "times" and "seasons" and the logion in Luke 9:26 links the Father with the future coming of the Son of Man. These references to the Father and the Son testify to the continuing role of the Father in a series of past and future events from the nativity story to the parousia of the Son of Man. Besides explicitly associating the Father with these events, these verses stress that God is the Father of the Son.

Although the Gospel of Luke contains five verses which identify God as the Father of the disciples, all five are in dominical logia taken from the evangelist's sources (6:36; 11:2, 13; 12:30, 32). Luke-Acts seems to place more emphasis on the identification of God as the Father of Jesus than on the identification of God as the Father of the disciples.

10

"Pentecost as a Recurrent Theme in Luke-Acts"

Earl Richard

This essay examines the crucial theme of the Spirit's manifestation in Jesus' ministry and the early community's activity.
While scholars have examined the pentecost episode of Acts 2
and recognized the importance of the Spirit for Luke,[1] it is
rarely noted that the pentecost experience is not limited to the
Jerusalem community. Indeed, new missionary endeavors and
other episodes are introduced with additional manifestations
of the Spirit.

1. The Spirit in Luke-Acts: Introductory Remarks

Contrary to popular perception, the appearance of the Spirit
is not frequent in Luke's Gospel. The term "spirit" appears as
follows: Matthew 19/12, Mark 23/6, Luke 36/18, and Acts
70/58 (occurrences of word and references to Holy Spirit,
respectively).[2] Of the eighteen uses of the term to refer to the
Spirit in Luke, eight occur in the infancy stories; of the ten
others, five are taken from Mark. These data agree with
Matthean usage; two appear in the infancy narratives and, of
the ten others, six are borrowed from Mark. The infancy
narratives aside, Matthew has added four and Luke five references to the Spirit. Therefore, it is not the frequency of the
theme but its function in Luke's Gospel which is crucial.

Acts presents a different situation; in a few cases the term
refers to evil or human spirits, but most refer to the Holy
Spirit. While they occur throughout, there is a concentration
of these in the first 13 chapters. These statistics indicate that

---

* Notes for Chapter 10 can be found on pp. 181-83

the Spirit plays an increasingly important role after Jesus' departure (frequency in Acts) and that the Spirit is crucial in understanding Luke's conception of beginnings (first part of Acts). Further, the other occurrences, while fewer in number, cluster around several themes: the Jewish and Gentile missions, Paul's ministry and role, and John and the baptism of the Spirit.

In more general terms the Spirit plays an important part in the implementation of what Luke sees as the divine plan for salvation.[3] It is the link between the Old Age and the New for it is that same Spirit which spoke through "the prophets of old." In the infancy narratives one sees particularly how the Spirit connects the time of Israel with that of God's visitation, for the prophetic figures who prepare for Jesus are imbued with the Spirit: John before birth, Elizabeth, Zechariah, Simeon, and Mary his mother.

Jesus' ministry is closely associated by Luke with the Spirit's activity; it comes down on him at baptism, leads him into the wilderness, and fills him with power. Also, Jesus is born by the Spirit's action, is said to be full of the Spirit, and initiates his mission because the Spirit is upon him. Without subordinating him to the Spirit (he is "led ... by the Spirit" not "driven out" as in Mark)[4] Luke stresses its influence on him.[5] Apart from the prophetic figures of the infancy stories, only Jesus receives the Spirit in the gospel. So it is both the agency of God's action in Jesus and the dynamism of his ministry.[6] But its role, foreannounced in the gospel, changes after Jesus' departure. The risen Lord becomes its sender and dispenser (Acts 2:33), for he now baptizes with the Spirit. Jesus bestows upon his followers the gift of the Spirit who will teach them what to say, allow them to speak God's word boldly, and guide the mission according to God's design.

2. The Spirit's Coming
Lexical, Thematic, and Temporal Study

Since the pentecost episode of Acts 2 is one of several manifestations of the Spirit, it is necessary to investigate all such passages to understand the theme's function in Luke-Acts.

The principal texts are: Acts 2 (Pentecost), 4:31 (community at prayer), 8:14f. (Samaritan mission), 10-11 (Cornelius episode), 19:1f. (John's disciples), and Luke 3:21-22 (Jesus' baptism). Also important are the Spirit's coming upon Mary (Luke 1:35), the prophetic figures and disciples who are "filled with the Spirit," and Paul's reception of the Spirit (Acts 9:17). Owing to its complexity and length, the pentecost episode is treated last and will serve to confirm our literary analysis.

Since the study focuses on the Spirit's manifestation, episodes presenting its coming or bestowal are examined lexically. Recurring vocabulary and subsidiary themes are noted and the repetitive character of the motif underscored. These phenomena confirm the theme's use as a leitmotif in Luke-Acts and indicate the author's preoccupation with temporal factors and their potential for providing unity to the story of Jesus and of the Jesus movement. The pentecost theme acquires an iterative character and function; that is, the Spirit's manifestations participate, by their repetitive features, in the paradigmatic pentecost experience and yet, through their unitive character, transcend this episode and represent the outpouring of the Spirit in the end-days. So the terms "temporal," "repetitive," "iterative," and "unitive" describe the role time plays in the narrative.[7]

ACTS 4:31—THE COMMUNITY AT PRAYER

> And when they had prayed, the place in which they were gathered together was shaken, and they were filled with the Holy Spirit and spoke the word of God with boldness.

The Spirit's coming in Luke-Acts is often placed in the context of prayer;[8] this is true of the pentecost, Samaritan, Cornelius, and Ephesian episodes, and of Jesus' baptism (an addition to Mark) and Paul's reception of the Spirit. As one gathers from the context, the theme of prayer has a special function in this episode. After presenting the disciples' trial and the resulting threats, Luke recalls that the roles of Herod and Pilate (Jew and Gentile) in the story are part of God's plan. So there is a request for boldness in the midst of threats, boldness which is granted with the Spirit's coming (4:29, 31). So the purpose of the episode is the granting of the Spirit who will give the disciples the boldness which God's design requires; one should remember Jesus' promise that the Father would give the Spirit to those who ask (Luke 11:13). The theme of prayer then serves an iterative function for Luke, since it provides narrative (i.e., repeated, concurrent action) and thematic unity to the pentecost episodes.

The community is said "to be filled with the Spirit," a favorite Lukan expression, for which *pimplēmi, plērēs,* and once *plēroō* are used interchangeably. Not only is this said of the pentecost community but also of Paul after his call and Jesus following his baptism (Luke 4:1; Acts 2:4; 9:17). Beyond this, many individuals in Acts and in the infancy narratives are also thus described in episodes which do not concern so much the Spirit's coming as its presence within human agents. With this recurrent phrase Luke expresses the result of the Spirit's manifestation and stresses its presence throughout salvation history.

Further, the locale of the episode is said "to shake." If this rare term only here relates to the Spirit's coming, its proximity to the pentecost episode with its physical signs and use of the expression "filled with the Spirit" indicate Luke's intention; this event is a repetition of the pentecost episode and its function is to stress the Spirit's role in the spreading and preaching of the good news "with boldness." Lastly, the theme of boldness is significant since it first appears following the Spirit's coming at Pentecost (2:28), occurs prominently in the conflict situations of chapter 4 (vv. 13, 29, 31), and closes Luke's work on an optimistic note (28:31, "with all boldness").[9]

ACTS 8:14-17—THE SAMARITAN MISSION

> Now when the apostles at Jerusalem heard that Samaria had received the word of God, they sent to them Peter and John who came down and prayed for them that they might receive the Holy Spirit; for it had not yet fallen on any of them, but they had only been baptized in the name of the Lord Jesus. Then they laid their hands on them and they received the Holy Spirit.

In this episode the theme of prayer is subordinate to the role of the Jerusalem church, another important Lukan theme, while the Spirit's coming is described by two new terms: "receive" (vv. 15, 17, 19) and "fall upon" (16). The latter is also employed thus in the Cornelius episode (10:44; 11:15); but despite its occurrence in only two pentecost episodes, Luke implies by Peter's words in 11:15 ("the Holy Spirit fell on them just as on us at the beginning") that the initial coming of the Spirit was also a "falling upon," that is, a similar or identical experience. So by the extension of the unusual term "fall upon," Luke provides further iterative unity to the major pentecost scenes: the pentecost, Samaria, and Cornelius narratives.

The second expression "receive" the Spirit occurs eight times in Acts, never in the gospel. Besides its three occurrences here, it also appears in the Cornelius and Ephesus stories. Its use in the former is crucial ("people who have received the Holy Spirit just as we have," 10:47), for Luke again interconnects pentecost narratives. Jesus is also said to have received the promise of the Spirit from the Father (Acts 2:33). In terms of the story, Luke here refers to Jesus' reception of the Spirit in baptism; but, in light of early tradition, the evangelist, in the context of the Ascension and implied enthronement, stresses Jesus' resurrection and role in the "giving" of the Spirit.[10]

Finally, several problems should be noted. The Samaritans are said to believe and to have been baptized but have not received the Spirit.[11] Even more perplexing is that they have "only been baptized in the name of the Lord Jesus" (v. 16), a text which seems to contradict Acts 2:38: "repent and be baptized every one of you in the name of Jesus Christ . . . and you shall receive the gift of the Holy Spirit." Lexically, there is no doubt that Luke views the Samaritans' faith as genuine,[12] but it is unclear why the Spirit has not been given in relation to baptism in Jesus' name and why the theme of the "laying on of hands" is introduced (for the latter, see also 9:17 and 19:6, the Pauline and Ephesian episodes). Also related to these problems is the role of the Jerusalem apostles.[13]

ACTS 10-11—THE CORNELIUS EPISODE

Initially we should note the dual character of the episode;

both Peter and Cornelius are at prayer and there are two recitations of the Spirit's coming. Also, prior to the first of these, there are two references to the Spirit: 10:19-20 where the Spirit is described as the initiator of the episode and 10:38 where it is said: "God anointed Jesus of Nazareth with the Holy Spirit and with power." For our study, however, the pertinent texts are as follows:

> While Peter was still saying this, the Holy Spirit fell on all who heard the word. And the believers from among the circumcised who came with Peter were amazed, because the gift of the Holy Spirit had been poured out even on the Gentiles. For they heard them speaking in tongues and extolling God. Then Peter declared, 'Can anyone forbid water for baptizing these people who have received the Holy Spirit just as we have?' And he commanded them to be baptized in the name of Jesus Christ (10:44-48).
>
> As I began to speak, the Holy Spirit fell on them just as on us at the beginning. And I remembered the word of the Lord, how he said, 'John baptized with water, but you shall be baptized with the Holy Spirit.' If then God gave the same gift to them as he gave to us when we believed in the Lord Jesus Christ, who was I that I could withstand God? (11:15-17).

Several terms are used for the Spirit's manifestation: "fall on," "receive," "pour out," "baptize with the Spirit," and "give a gift to," the first two of which were noted in earlier texts. "Pour out" is rare in Luke and, as related to the Spirit, occurs only here and at Pentecost. Luke draws the term from the latter episode where it appears twice in the Joel citation: "I will pour out my Spirit" (Acts 2:17, 18). Later within Peter's speech Jesus' bestowal of the Spirit is described as "pouring out what you see and hear" (2:33). The term, therefore, and its accompanying stress on miraculous phenomena in Acts 2:8 ("seeing and hearing signs," though without the term "pouring out"), and 10 makes clear the generic unity of the main pentecost episodes.

While the theme of "baptizing with the Spirit" is important for the Synoptic tradition generally, it is more so for Luke who records the "baptism with the Spirit" saying on three different occasions: once in the mouth of John (Luke 3:16) and twice as dominical sayings (Acts 1:5; 11:16). Further, Luke uses a modified version of the saying in the last pentecost episode of Acts, the Ephesian pericope (19:4). We will return to the role John plays in Luke's conception of baptism and the manifestation of the Spirit.

Finally, the theme of "the giving of the Spirit" requires some attention. God, not Jesus, is said to give the Spirit (Acts 5:32; 15:8) or to give the gift (understood as the Spirit, 11:17) or else passive or impersonal expressions are employed for the bestowing of the Spirit or to refer to the Spirit as gift (2:38; 8:18; 10:45). Furthermore, a Q saying is modified as follows: "how much more will the heavenly Father give the Holy Spirit to those who ask him" (Luke 11:13; Matt 7:11 reads "good things"). God, therefore, is the giver, though once Jesus has received the Spirit, it is he who pours it out on those who believe (Acts 2:33). Thus, the theme of the divine giving or gift of the Spirit also appears in Acts 2, 8, and 10-11, and its iterative character is emphasized in 15:8 by Peter: "God ... giving them the Holy Spirit just as he did to us."

Additionally, several themes and problems should be noted. Speaking in tongues occurs in three scenes: the pentecost, Cornelius, and Ephesus episodes, and again Luke relates the Spirit's coming to the Jerusalem authorities (10:45; 11:2, 18). While in the Samaritan episode the baptism in Jesus' name (negatively presented) occurs before the reception of the Spirit (by the laying on of hands), in the Cornelius episode the manifestation of the Spirit precedes baptism in Jesus' name (positively presented). Further, the Spirit's coming occurs while Peter is preaching, not as a result of prayer, laying on of hands, or through baptism. It is also significant that the Spirit's coming to the Gentiles is related to that which occurred earlier to the Jerusalem community (10:47; 11:15, 17; 15:8). Finally, employing understatement, Luke insists, in the words of Peter ("who was I that I could withstand God?") that the granting of the Spirit is part of the divine plan.

ACTS 19:1-6—THE DISCIPLES OF JOHN AT EPHESUS

And he said to them: "Did you receive the Holy Spirit when

you believed?" And they said, "No, we have never even
heard that there is a Holy Spirit." And he said, "Into what
then were you baptized?" They said, "Into John's baptism."
And Paul said, "John baptized with baptism of repentance,
telling the people to believe in the one who was to come
after him, that is, Jesus." On hearing this, they were baptized
in the name of the Lord Jesus. And when Paul had laid his
hands upon them, the Holy Spirit came on them; and they
spoke with tongues and prophesied.

In this episode "receive" is again used when inquiring about
the Spirit's coming, though a new term, "come upon"
(*erchomai epi*), is employed. The same phrase (with a redun-
dant prefix, *eperchomai epi*) announces the Spirit's coming
both on Mary (Luke 1:35) and the apostles (Acts 1:8). Again
there occur the speaking in tongues and the laying on of hands
to confer the Spirit. Luke employs the saying about John's
baptism though the stress is not on baptism but belief in
John's successor. Luke introduces the theme of prophecy,
clearly relating this narrative to the Joel citation of the pentecost episode (Acts 2:17-18) and the gospel scene where
Zechariah prophesies about his prophet-like son (Luke 1:64,
67).

Lastly, a few problems should be noted. The term "disciple"
in Acts regularly refers to Christian believers; however, in 19:1
the people involved are John's disciples. Further, there is the
curious ignorance of the Spirit's existence. Also, there is some
disjointedness in the text, for the disciples are baptized in
Jesus' name and are granted the Spirit after the laying on of
hands (vv. 4, 6).

LUKE 3:21-22—JESUS' BAPTISM

Now when all the people were baptized, and when Jesus
also had been baptized and was praying, the heaven was
opened, and the Holy Spirit descended upon him in bodily
form, as a dove, and a voice came from heaven, "Thou art
my beloved Son; with thee I am well pleased."

Luke mentions no agent for the baptism, but instead has John imprisoned prior to Jesus' baptism, a fact which Conzelmann employed to defend his situating John in the age of Israel. Apart from the difficulties raised by this thesis,[14] it is preferable to appeal to Luke's tendency to round off episodes even when this creates narrative problems. But there is a more basic reason for this modification. The people and Jesus have been baptized and he is at prayer. In this way, Luke, deemphasizes John's water baptism (past tense)[15] and stresses the episode's theophanic or pentecost character (present tense): prayer, opening of heaven, descent of the Spirit, the heavenly voice, sonship, and servanthood. The stress on the physical nature of the episode (bodily form as a dove, heaven opened, voice) has its closest analogue in the pentecost event (Acts 2:1-4).[16] The term for the Spirit's coming, "descent," is traditional and is retained, for it, along with the heavenly voice, emphasizes that the Spirit comes from the heavenly Father. Here as elsewhere (announcement to Mary, two dominical sayings, and Acts 2:33 about the Father's promise), the Spirit is connected with Jesus' sonship.

Finally, the context of this scene is instructive for understanding its pentecost character. Even John is said to preach the good news (saying unique to Luke, 3:18), a message which the reader understands as announcing Jesus who "will baptize ... with the Holy Spirit and with fire" (v. 16). Jesus then, after submitting to water baptism,[17] undergoes baptism of the Spirit and in Acts is said to "pour out" (2:33) fire and Spirit (2:3-4). Thus, "the Baptist [in 3:16] is made to anticipate an event that, from Luke's perspective, had happened and continued to happen (Acts 2:1-4; 4:31; 8:14-17; 10:44-48; 11:15-18; 19:1-7)."[18]

OTHER PASSAGES

Several prophetic figures in the *infancy narratives* are imbued with the Spirit: John the Baptist, Elizabeth, and Zechariah (1:15, 41, 67). Further, there is the prophetic witness of Simeon of whom it is said, "the Holy Spirit was upon him" (2:25). Also, Mary is given the promise that the Spirit (also described as "the power of the Most High") will come upon her and that she will bear God's Son (1:35). Of added importance is this sonship theme and its relation to the heavenly voice of the baptism scene.

A word should also be said about *Acts 9:10-19* and its pentecost character. While Paul is at prayer, Ananias is sent by Jesus to lay hands on him, heal him, and cause him to be filled with the Spirit. Paul is then healed and baptized. As in the case of Mary (Luke 1:35), there is no actualization of the Spirit's coming though Luke in both cases hints at its fulfilment. In the first, Jesus' birth follows and later the heavenly voice confirms his sonship, whereas, in the second, Paul engages in extensive missionary activity after which Luke comments that the church was multiplied "in the comfort of the Holy Spirit" (9:31).

Followers are said to be *"filled with the Spirit"*: disciples at Pentecost, at prayer, Peter, the Seven, Stephen, and Barnabas—all in the first 13 chapters of Acts.

ACTS 2:1ff.—THE PENTECOST EPISODE

This passage is the most important, but since, by design, the pentecost themes were extracted from other passages, our task is simplified. The context of the Spirit's manifestation is that of prayer (1:14, 24) and apostolic preaching. First, however, we must deal with the episode's peculiarities. If only Acts 2 stresses the physical apocalyptic signs of the Spirit's coming (sudden sound from heaven like rushing wind and tongues of fire), there are also such physical, heavenly signs at Jesus' baptism and in Acts 4:31 (the place of assembly shakes). Also, while the speaking in tongues is emphasized in Acts 2, the same phenomenon occurs in the Cornelius and Ephesian pentecost pericopes. Only here, however, is the phenomenon interpreted as foreign languages, i.e., xenoglossy[19] rather than glossolalia. Further, Acts 2 stresses the universalism of the Spirit's manifestation (vv. 5, 9-11). Also, the theme of prophecy (relation to the Spirit), the eschatological nature of the believing community (Joel citation), the roles of Father, Jesus/Son, and that of the Spirit are carefully explicitated in the Lukan narrative.

Secondly, this narrative introduces most of the terms employed in other episodes about the Spirit's manifestation: "filled with the Spirit," "speak in tongues," "prophesy," "pour out," "receive," "promise or gift of the Spirit," "baptize in Jesus' name." These graphic terms function as a semantic field in establishing the paradigmatic character of this pentecost episode. Thus, the repeated use of these terms in subsequent narratives creates for the reader a sense of thematic continuity and suggests a unitive function for the original pentecost story.

3. Function of the Pentecost Theme in the Lukan Plan

Having discerned Luke's terminology and the principal themes associated with the granting of the Spirit, we now examine the function of the episodes in the Lukan narrative.

CHRISTIAN BEGINNINGS

In Christian tradition the paradigmatic manifestation of the Spirit has always been the pentecost episode. It is no surprise, therefore, that this event is associated with the beginning of the community. Since, as our study shows, there are several pentecost experiences recounted during the course of the mission, we need to reexamine the question of Christian origins in Luke's narrative.

There are several missionary beginnings in Acts: the mission to the Jews, Samaritans, and Gentiles. Luke has designed three "major" pentecost passages to establish the principal missions of the early church. The Jerusalem story is directed to the establishing of the Jewish mission, for the reader is told that the audience of the speech consists of Jerusalem Jews, Judaeans, and all Jerusalemites (2:5, 14). While this passage bears a universalist emphasis ("men from every nation under heaven," "Jews and proselytes," the list of nations), it also introduces the Jewish mission. When Jesus' followers begin preaching to their fellow Jews, the Spirit plays a central role in relation both to the preachers (2:1-4) and to the audience (2:38).

The Samaritan episode, which opens up a new mission field, also is put under the aegis of the Spirit. As the Spirit was given to the Jews so is it to the new converts, the Samaritans.

The same is true about the entry of the Gentiles into the community; the Spirit comes on them just as it did on the Jewish followers in Jerusalem. The pentecost theme then is employed to authenticate the various Christian beginnings, whether Jewish, Samaritan, or Gentile.

Also, in all three Peter and the twelve are involved in the opening of mission areas: Peter as member of the group at Pentecost where he has the task of delivering the pentecost speech, Peter along with John in Samaria, and Peter as the central character of the Cornelius episode. The context is the symbolic role which Jerusalem plays in Luke-Acts. Luke focuses on Peter as spokesman for the twelve, that unique, reconstituted group of the beginnings. The mission fields are related to Jesus through the witness of the twelve, one of their major functions in Acts. In this way the pentecost episodes authenticate the missions and establish continuity between the churches and the risen Lord.[20] Even the establishment of Antioch as the base for the world mission is authenticated by a Jerusalem envoy, Barnabas, whom Luke pointedly says is "full of the Holy Spirit" (11:24).

Further, as the pentecost episode marks the beginning of the preaching to Jews and soon the mission runs into major opposition or threats (2:1; 4:29-31), so the Cornelius narrative shows a similar pattern:[21] first the successful preaching to Gentiles and the arrival of the Spirit, then a threat to the Gentile mission from the circumcision party (10, 11). In the first case, Luke presents a manifestation of the Spirit as a resolution of the threat. Thus, in 4:31 as a result of the Spirit's coming, the disciples in response to Jewish threats preach the word of God with boldness. In the second, Peter recounts in slightly different form the encounter with Cornelius, since the circumcision party has condemned his action in Antioch (11:2). After Peter tells them how the Spirit came in spite of him, Luke terminates the episode with words from the circumcision party: "Then to the Gentiles also God has granted repentance unto life" (11:18). So Luke uses the pentecost theme to resolve theologically the ideological and historical problems of the storyline. Even the Samaritan episode would gain from such a perspective, that is, recognizing two stages in the narrative: one concerning baptism and another about the conferring of the Spirit.

STRUCTURE OF ACTS

Acts 1:8b provides Luke's temporal and geographic plan: first a Jerusalem ministry, then a Samaritan and Judaean ministry in chapters 8ff., and from 13ff. a world mission extending to Rome.[22] Of interest to us is the Spirit theme and its relation to this plan. The Jerusalem ministry revolves around the pentecost episodes of Acts 2 and 4:31, while the next mission relates to the Spirit's activity in Samaria and Judaea (chap 8). Finally, the world-wide mission finds its preparation in Paul's reception of the Spirit (9:17), finds its raison d'être in the Cornelius episode (chaps 10, 11) and its impetus in the Spirit's activity: choice during worship of Paul and Barnabas for the world mission (13:1-3). Luke has structured the narrative of Acts so that the Spirit and the pentecost theme provide the link between the Christian mission and the divine plan; Jews, Gentiles, Samaritans, people far away, Roman citizens have become followers of Jesus and the movement is open to all who call upon his name. Indeed, God employs agents, especially Jesus and, in his stead, the Spirit,[23] so that ultimately things happen not because of human plans or activity but because they correspond to God's design.

THE KERYGMATIC SPEECHES AND THE COMING OF THE SPIRIT

The first half of Acts contains six kerygmatic speeches, five by Peter, one by Paul (chaps 2, 3, 4, 5, 10, 13), which bear a brief account of Jesus' life and death. Also, it is commonly admitted that these are Lukan compositions. It is significant that four involve pentecost episodes and that the other two are specifically related to the Spirit's activity. In this way the link between christology and the Spirit's activity is emphasized, for as Luke puts it: Jesus, "having received from the Father the promise of the Holy Spirit, has poured out this which you see and hear" (Acts 2:23). Jesus is God's agent and visitation; but as "absent" Lord, he bestows the Spirit and operates through it. The Spirit is a gift from God (even to Jesus) and, after Jesus' departure and in his name, it is the believer's teacher and source of power. Thus, the Spirit is subordinate to Jesus for it acts in his behalf and continues his work.[24]

THE COMING OF THE SPIRIT: PARALLELS BETWEEN LUKE AND ACTS

Both volumes begin with promises of the Spirit's coming, first to Mary (Luke 1:35) and then to the apostles (Acts 1:4-5, 8); also both in subsequent chapters and in graphic terms recite its bestowal: the baptism and pentecost events. The gospel tells of the Spirit's descent on Jesus, who in the gospel subsequently will be the only person "full of the Spirit." The bestowal of the Spirit in Jesus' case underscores Luke's concept of Jesus' identity and function. There is only one agent and servant of God, that is, Jesus who is given the Spirit of sonship and servanthood by the Father (as "Spirit" and "power," Luke 1:35). In Acts, Jesus becomes the dispenser of the Spirit in the Father's stead; the Spirit is received by many and on many occasions, for its role is that of mediator in Jesus' name. The Spirit's role in Jesus' life is a once only situation as was the life of *the* prophet and *the* servant; its role in the community's life, however, is manifold and continuous. The parallels between the baptism of Jesus and the subsequent Nazareth programmatic speech, on the one hand, and between the pentecost episode, the following speech, and the remaining complex of the spirit theme in Acts, on the other hand, could be examined further, but here I would underscore Luke's thematic use of the Spirit to construct the beginnings of the gospel and Acts so as to present a new christological and ecclesiological vision.

There are differences, however, between them in this regard. As noted earlier, Luke's treatment of the Spirit in the two volumes is different statistically. Also, the pentecost episodes of Acts are closer in terminology and narrative structure to one another than they are to Jesus' baptism. If the baptism and pentecost scenes are obviously parallel in Luke's schema, they are nonetheless dissimilar in terminology. There are reasons for this: the use of the Markan baptism story (thus redactional restraint), the acceptance of the Spirit's traditional role, and the conviction that Jesus' experience was unique. However, I am led to see the increased and modified role given the Spirit in the infancy narratives and in Acts as owing to a later development in Luke's narrative project and theology.[25]

BAPTISM WITH THE SPIRIT OR THE ROLE OF JOHN IN LUKE-ACTS

The episode about John's disciples (Acts 19:1-7) is puzzling; why does Luke present this episode so late in Acts and make it the last narrative manifestation of the Spirit? Why also, prior to this, is Apollos presented as learned in scripture, baptized only in John's baptism, yet as one in the Spirit who teaches accurately about Jesus? Such queries are clarified by a study of John's role in Luke-Acts. Luke begins the gospel with John, has him announce a baptism not with water but one by Jesus with the Spirit (3:16), and repeats the "baptism with the Spirit" saying on three occasions: at the beginning of Acts (1:5), during the Cornelius episode (11:16), and in Acts 19:4.[26] In the last, Luke insists that John's baptism is not sufficient for he "told the people to believe in the one who was to come after him, that is, Jesus." There follow baptism, the Spirit's coming, and pentecost phenomena. As the Spirit comes after the twelve are reconstituted, so Luke, after presenting the Spirit's manifestation on John's disciples, concludes: "There were about twelve of them in all" (19:7).

Two areas need clarification: John's role in the gospel and the part he plays in Acts. 1) In an interesting addition to a Q saying about John as more than a prophet and about the least in the kingdom being greater than he, Luke presents the roles which John's baptism and the Spirit's coming have in the divine scheme: "when they heard this all ... justified God, having been baptized with the baptism of John; but the Pharisees and the lawyers rejected the purpose of God for themselves, not having been baptized by him" (Luke 7:29-30). John and the Spirit have roles in God's plan of salvation in Jesus' name; John's role is preparatory, while that of the Spirit persists.[27]

2) If the gospel's references to John tend to remain faithful to Markan and Q usage, the increased attention to him in the infancy narratives and Acts is noteworthy, owing to Luke's concerted effort to subjugate him to Jesus in the pre-ministry stories, to modify the beginning of the public ministry to separate Jesus' reception of the Spirit from John's water baptism, and to give a prominent role in Acts to John's activity

and disciples. On the one hand, J.A. Fitzmyer, in discussing Jesus' submission to John's baptism, suggests that "the evangelists portray Jesus as a sort of disciple of John, accepting his baptism as a mark of initial association with him and recognizing it as a preparatory stage of his own ministry."[28] On the other hand, A. George concludes from his analysis of the Ephesian episode that "it probably signals the passage of the Johannine community into the one Church."[29] Thus, I am led to suggest a recognition on Luke's part of some of the realities of the Jesus movement; namely, that, while its origins reached in part to John (Acts 1:22; 10:37; 13:24), tradition steadily maintained the centrality of the Christ-event and the movement desired union with its Baptist fellow believers (19:1-2).[30] In symbolic terms the reunion involves a new pentecost and the prophetic activity of twelve followers of John, as a parallel to Acts 1-2.[31]

4. Some Concluding Observations

Luke uses the pentecost theme to define the parallels between master and disciples, to present the unfolding of the divine plan, and to trace the missionary activity of the "absent" Lord and his witnesses. Luke, a third-generation Christian, is convinced that God is still at work, seeking what is lost. This theme of God's seeking out humans is seen by Luke in relation to God's eternal plan, promised through the prophets, realized in a special visitation, and now being carried out through other agents. The Spirit for Luke is a pervading reality throughout this divine schema, whose presence accounts for the origin, life, and mission of the community, and which grants the believer boldness, comfort, and peace until the Lord's return (Acts 3:20-21).

Thus, Pentecost for Luke, is a paradigmatic episode that, in parallel with Jesus' reception of the Spirit, signals conferral of power for and the beginning of the mission and witness to the ends of the earth. It is likewise an iterative theme that marks the stages of God's dealings with humanity (beginning with "the prophets of old"), that initiates the movement's beginnings (Jewish, Samaritan, and Gentile), that signals the stages of the community's growth, unity, and mission (expansion, unity, Pauline role), and that emphasizes Luke's agency christology whereby Jesus first receives the Spirit and then "pours out" the Spirit upon all who seek, repent, and are baptized in his name.[32] Finally, Pentecost, owing to its unitive presentation, is proof of God's pouring out of the Spirit upon all flesh in the last days, first upon Jesus and then upon "all the lowly who would follow him to glory."[33]

11

The Non-Roman Opponents of Paul

Richard J. Cassidy

Within Acts Luke presents Paul experiencing opposition on a wide variety of fronts. According to Luke's reports, Paul faced opposition from members of the Christian community who were dedicated to the full observance of the Jewish Law. He also faced life-threatening opposition from Gentiles who were threatened by the implications of his message, from Jews of the Diaspora and Jews in Jerusalem who refused to believe in his message, and from the chief priests and their Sanhedrin allies.

While a general knowledge concerning all five types of opposition serves to promote an appreciation for the arduous ministry that Luke portrays Paul conducting in Acts, an in-depth knowledge concerning the latter four types of opposition has particular value with respect to the interpretation of other Acts passages in which Paul is portrayed interacting with Roman military and political officials. Accordingly, it will be the principal task of the present essay to make a detailed analysis of the opposition that Paul received from each of the latter four "non-Roman" groups.[1] This analysis having been completed, a qualified hypothesis relative to the subject of the Lukan Paul's compatibility with Roman rule will then be suggested.

1. Gentiles in Asia Minor and Greece

In describing Paul's journeys during the middle chapters of Acts, Luke indicates that Paul twice experienced significant opposition from Gentiles whose economic livelihood was undermined by his teaching and activity. In the first, at Phillippi, Paul expelled a divining spirit from a servant girl

* Notes for Chapter 11 can be found on pp. 183-85

and thus deprived her masters of the source of their income. Luke reports that their response was to drag Paul and Silas into the marketplace and denounce them before the city's magistrates (16:16-19).

Remarkably, the charges which the girl's masters made against Paul and Silas went far beyond the deed of exorcism. Luke relates that they specifically denounced the two disciples for being Jews and for being disturbers of the public order: "These men are Jews and they are disturbing our city. They advocate customs which it is not lawful for us Romans to accept or practice" (16:20-21).

As a result of this public denunciation, other Gentiles joined the girl's masters in their attack upon Paul and so too did the magistrates. Luke indicates that, as a consequence, Paul and Silas were severely beaten and thrown into prison (16:22-23).

As a result of his rejection of idols, Paul also experienced serious opposition from Gentile opponents at Ephesus. Luke portrays Demetrius raising a public outcry against Paul and engendering much confusion and indignation among the populace of the city (19:24-29). Although his report is not totally clear in this regard, Luke seems to indicate that some Jews of the city were also on the verge of being attacked by the crowd which gathered.[2]

Following counsel from his own disciples and some of the Asiarchs, Paul did not enter the town theater and was not a part of the tumultuous events that took place there. As Luke describes the situation, the town clerk played a decisive role in alleviating the crowd's concerns and reassuring them regarding the vitality of the Artemis cult. As a result, no personal harm came to any of those who were present, nor did any harm subsequently come to Paul himself (19:35-41).[3]

In chapter fourteen Luke records two other instances in which Gentiles were involved in efforts against Paul. In both of these cases, however, Paul's initial adversaries were unbelieving Jews. Rejecting Paul's message themselves, they conspired among the Gentiles and (in one case) among the rulers so that Paul himself might be destroyed.

Luke first reports that the unbelieving Jews at Iconium so poisoned the minds of the Gentiles against Paul that the city became divided with some of the populace opposing Paul and

Barnabas and some supporting them (14:2-4). He then relates that "an attempt was made by both Gentiles and Jews, with their rulers, to molest them and stone them" (14:5).[4]

In comparison, when he describes the situation that developed later at Lystra, Luke indicates that Gentiles were less centrally involved in the action against Paul although the action itself inflicted greater harm upon him. According to 14:19-20, unbelieving Jews from Pisidian Antioch and Iconium came to Lystra and stoned Paul so severely that they left him for dead. Inasmuch as Luke states that they attacked Paul after "having persuaded the people" (14:9), he also seemingly indicates that the (Gentile) townspeople of Lystra had at least some level of involvement in this attempted assassination.[5]

2. The "Unbelieving" Jews of the Diaspora

Luke portrays Paul achieving considerable success in preaching among the Jews who were dispersed in various cities and locations outside of Jerusalem and Judaea. Nevertheless, along with the converts that he made in the Jewish communities he visited, Luke also reports that Paul frequently encountered serious opposition.

Luke only once explicitly uses the term, "unbelieving," as an adjective characterizing those Jews who rejected Paul's message.[6] However, the understanding that those who oppose Paul do so because they are unbelieving with respect to his message is implicit in virtually all of the other passages in which Luke portrays Paul experiencing hostility from Jews. And for this reason, as well as for the consideration that Christian interpreters need be scrupulously careful in differentiating between the various kinds of "Jewish" responses that Luke portrays,[7] this adjective will be consistently used to describe Paul's opponents within the Diaspora and (apart from the special case of the high priest and the Sanhedrin officials) also within Jerusalem itself.

In all there are fully twelve instances in which Luke portrays Paul experiencing hostility from Jewish groups of the Diaspora. In five of these instances the unbelieving Jews of the particular place actually seek to kill Paul.[8] In four other instances they oppose him so strongly that he is forced to leave town.[9] In addition, Luke also describes two cases in which the opposition manifested does not greatly influence Paul[10] and one case (the Jewish magician, Bar-Jesus on Cyprus) in which Paul actually overcomes the unbelieving Jew who opposes him.

Describing events that occurred right after Paul's conversion, Luke reports that the Jews who lived in Damascus reacted to Paul's demonstration that Jesus was the Christ by plotting to kill him. Indeed, Paul was only able to escape their hands by having his disciples lower him over the city wall in a basket by night (9:23-24).

Similarly, after Paul returned to Jerusalem, his bold preaching and his disputes with "the Hellenists" resulted in the members of this group wanting to kill him (9:28-29). Luke does not indicate precisely who comprised this latter group but various factors suggest that he understood it to be composed of Greek-speaking Jews, formerly resident in the Diaspora, but now living in Jerusalem.[11] Luke states that the Jerusalem disciples took the Hellenists' machinations so seriously that they brought Paul out of Jerusalem to Caesarea and sent him on a ship to Tarsus (9:30).

Later on, at Cyprus, Paul did not receive opposition from Jews in any of the synagogues that he visited, but the Jewish false prophet, Bar-Jesus, did seek to obstruct his preaching to Sergius Paulus, the proconsul (13:6-8).

At Pisidian Antioch, jealous of his initial success among the Jewish community there, some Jews rejected Paul's message and began to oppose and revile him (13:45). They eventually organized "devout women of high standing and the leading men of the city"[12] to drive Paul and Barnabas out of the district. The two disciples left, shaking the dust from their feet in protest (13:50-51).

According to Luke's narrative the coalition organized by the unbelieving Jews of Iconium was, if anything, even more formidable than that at Antioch. A "great company" of Jews accepted Paul's message, but as noted in the preceding section, those that did not stirred up the Gentiles of the city and succeeded in dividing the public opinion regarding Paul. Eventually the unbelieving Jews, along with the Gentiles they had influenced and their rulers, made plans to stone Paul and Barnabas. However, upon learning of this, the two missionaries fled the city (14:5-6).

It was following this at Lystra that Paul came closest to death at the hands of his opponents. Initially he received much support from the populace. However, as noted previously, Luke then indicates that some of the unbelieving Jews from Pisidian Antioch as well as Iconium arrived on the scene and turned the situation against Paul. Luke provides only the sparsest description of what occurred at this point: " . . . and having persuaded the people, they stoned Paul and dragged him out of the city supposing he was dead" (14:19). Paul was not dead, however. He was eventually able to walk back into the city and the next day left with Barnabas for Derbe (14:20).

Later in his narrative Luke portrays unbelieving Jews from Thessalonica opposing Paul with almost as much diligence as those from Pisidian Antioch and Iconium. In their own city these Jews, jealous of Paul, manipulated some local trouble-makers, gathered a crowd, and set the city in an uproar (17:5). These same Jews then followed Paul to Beroea and incited the crowds against him to such a degree that he was eventually obliged to sail for Athens (17:13-15).

Later at Corinth, Paul once again encountered intense hostility from those Jews who rejected his message. Luke portrays him shaking out his garments against them and moving the base of his activities to a neighboring house that was owned by a receptive "God-worshiper" (18:6-7). Luke also reports that Paul's Jewish opponents made a united attack upon him a year and a half later, bringing him before the Roman proconsul. However, the proconsul refused to take action against him, and in this instance Paul came to no harm (18:12-18).

At the end of chapter eighteen, Luke reports that Paul stopped for a period at Ephesus and "argued with the Jews" there (18:19). Later, within the context of Paul's return to that city, Luke indicates more explicitly that some members of Paul's Jewish audience "were stubborn and disbelieved, speaking evil of the Way before the congregation . . . " (19:9). Luke reports that Paul deemed it advisable to withdraw from the synagogue to a neighboring lecture hall in the light of this opposition.

Prior to his last journey to Jerusalem, the final passage in which Luke portrays unbelieving Jews opposing Paul's efforts comes at 20:2-3 when Paul is in Greece. Luke relates that a group of unbelieving Jews plotted against Paul just as he was about to set sail for Syria. As a consequence he was forced to alter his plans and went to Troas by a land journey through Macedonia (20:4-5).

Mention was made above concerning the activities of certain "Asian Jews" against Paul in Jerusalem. Since Luke literally describes this group as "the Jews from Asia" (21:27), it is a matter of speculation whether he understood these Jews to be Paul's opponents from the recent or distant past.[13] What is clear from his account at this point is that these Jews remember and recognize Paul when they see him in Jerusalem. In fact, in attempting to rally the populace of Jerusalem against Paul, they infer that they themselves have personal knowledge of Paul's subversive activities:[14]

> "Men of Israel, help! This is the man who is teaching men everywhere against the people and the law and this place; moreover he has brought Greeks into the temple, and he has defiled this holy place" (21:28).

The next verse in Luke's account indicates that the spark which fired their outburst against Paul was actually a fiction of their own imaginations: they had seen Trophimus the Ephesian with Paul in the city and had leapt to the conclusion that Paul must have brought him into the temple as well. Nevertheless, their anger against Paul is such that they want to kill him then and there. Luke's description at this point depicts a scene of great chaos. Having taken hold of Paul (21:27), the Asian Jews succeed in arousing a large crowd of people. Paul is dragged out into the city proper and the gates of the temple are quickly shut. A riotous uproar ensues (21:30-31).[15]

Luke next reports that the Roman tribune, Lysias, responding to the threat of a riot, extricates Paul from his attackers (21:31-36). From this point forward in the narrative, Paul remains in Roman custody. This does not mean, however, that he is free from further attacks by unbelieving Jews. While nothing more is heard regarding machinations against him by unbelieving Jews from the territory of Asia or elsewhere in the Diaspora,[16] Paul must still face great threats from the unbelieving Jews of Jerusalem and particularly from the high priest and those associated with him on the Sanhedrin.

3. The "Unbelieving" Jews of Jerusalem

In describing the response which followed their outcry, Luke indicates that the Asian Jews struck a responsive chord with the larger Jewish populace. Then "all the city was aroused, and the people ran together; they seized Paul and dragged him out of the temple, and at once the gates were shut" (21:30) is his description of the resulting scene.

Initially it is not clear whether those joining against Paul are doing so because they accepted the report that he had profaned the temple, because they gave credence to the charge that he had been teaching everywhere "against the people and the law and this place," or for a combination of these factors. Whatever their exact concerns, the crowd which gathered manifested a furious violence against Paul:

> And when he came to the steps, he was actually carried by the soldiers because of the violence of the crowd; for the mob of the people followed, crying, "Away with him!" (21:35-36).

Subsequently, by virtue of the fact that he began to address them in Hebrew, Paul succeeded in temporarily pacifying the mob (21:22). However, Luke indicates that a highly controversial item in Paul's address rekindled all of their hostility toward him. When Paul quoted the Lord's instruction to him concerning his mission to the Gentiles, the crowd reacted in the following manner:

> Up to this word they listened to him; then they lifted up their voices and said, "Away with such a fellow from the earth! For he ought not to live," And ... they cried out and waved their garments and threw dust into the air (21:22-23a).

Clearly the sense of Luke's account is that the gathered crowd would not accept any words of Jesus as justification for a mission among the Gentiles. Luke's description does not precisely indicate whether the crowd's outrage flowed exclusively from Paul's advertence to the mission he had undertaken among the Gentiles or whether their fury should also be understood as having arisen from other factors as well. Luke may mean to indicate that the crowd now believed all of the charges against Paul and considered him not only an apostate Jew but also a positive threat to Judaism's central institutions.[17]

It is at this point in the proceedings that Luke portrays an event in which still another group of Paul's enemies emerges. The tribune brought Paul to a hearing before the Jerusalem Sanhedrin and thus into contact with Ananias, the high priest, and those allied with him. As the situation developed, this group manifested intense and violent hostility toward Paul. Nevertheless, the tribune extricated Paul from the melee and brought him back to the relative safety of the Roman barracks (23:1-10).

Such an outcome did not prevent the most zealous of Paul's unbelieving opponents from proceeding further against him, however. By Luke's account forty of them put themselves under oath not to eat or drink until they had killed him. Their plan was to ambush Paul outside of the barracks and they urged the chief priests and their allies to request that Paul be brought to the Sanhedrin for an additional hearing on his case (23:12-15).

Inasmuch as it is manifestly the sense of the Acts narrative that the chief priests themselves viewed such a development favorably, there is a certain convergence between both groups of Paul's opponents at this point. While the following excerpt from Paul's nephew's report to the tribune indicates only that "the Jews" had agreed to petition for another Sanhedrin meeting, it is clear from the context that both groups are included in this reference. The chief priests and their allies on the Sanhedrin are, in effect, co-conspirators with certain other "unbelieving" Jews in a bold attempt to secure Paul's death:

> And he said, "The Jews have agreed to ask you to bring Paul down to the council tomorrow, as though they were

going to inquire somewhat more closely about him. But do not yield to them; for more than forty of their men lie in ambush for him, having bound themselves by an oath neither to eat nor drink till they have killed him; and now they are ready, waiting for the promise from you" (23:20-21).

4. The Chief Priests and Their Sanhedrin Allies

Before examining the range of measures which Luke now portrays the chief priests and their Sanhedrin allies undertaking against Paul, it is well to review the record of their contacts with him up until this point in the narrative. At the outset it should be noted that, previous to the time of Paul's sharp controversy with the high priest during his Sanhedrin hearing, Luke has portrayed Paul standing in alliance *with* the chief priests *against* the disciples of Jesus.

The first passage in Acts which depicts Paul standing together with the chief priests and other members of the Sanhedrin is that in which the circumstances of Stephen's execution are detailed. There, Luke not only reports that Saul took care of the garments of those who stoned Stephen (7:58), he also states: "And Saul was consenting to his death" (8:1a). The significance of this latter note concerning Paul's attitude should not be underestimated. By it, Luke portrays Paul agreeing with the Sanhedrin members that Stephen's activities and words could not be tolerated and agreeing with them that death by stoning was the way to put an end to them.

In the second set of reports which bear upon his prior relationship with the chief priests and their associates, Paul is portrayed in still closer relationship with them. In 8:1b Luke implies that those who murdered Stephen were then responsible for a more general persecution against the Jerusalem church, and in 8:3 he portrays Saul participating in this persecution and actually playing a central role in it. Then in 9:1 Luke indicates that Paul himself thought of extending the persecution to disciples in Damascus and went to the high priest for letters authorizing him to do so. Within Luke's portrait of his activities, the fact that Paul received approval for this initiative implies that he had emerged as a dedicated and trusted ally of the chief priests and was no longer to be regarded merely as the young custodian of their cloaks.

It is against this background of Paul's previous association with the chief priests that Luke portrays him addressing the angry Jerusalem crowd. Although a considerable amount of time has elapsed between the time of Paul's mission to Damascus in chapter nine and his presence before the mob in Jerusalem in chapter twenty-two, Paul still presumes to tell the crowd that "the high priest and the whole council of elders"[18] will bear witness to him. Paul describes his previous collaboration with them ("from them I received letters") and seems to suggest to the crowd that the chief priests' prior knowledge of Paul will give them a basis for speaking on his behalf (22:5).

Luke's description of the attitude with which Paul approached his initial hearing before the Sanhedrin shows him proceeding in a similarly positive manner. Luke does not portray him as in any way reluctant to appear before that body.[19] And, once there, Paul begins straightforwardly to explain that he has operated in good conscience in all that he has done, past and present alike. Seemingly, Paul expects to be able to persuade the Sanhedrin members concerning the validity of the path he has followed since the time of his conversion.

Just how mistaken Paul was in thinking that he could now receive a favorable hearing from his former allies is clearly revealed by the slap on the mouth that Luke describes him receiving at the high priest's instruction. Luke then describes a situation which deteriorates so rapidly that the Roman tribune's intervention is necessary to prevent Paul from being torn limb from limb (23:2-10).

From this point forward Luke portrays the high priest and his allies using a variety of strategies in trying to achieve Paul's death. Initially, they willingly abet the plot of "the forty" to ambush Paul (23:15, 20). That plot being foiled by the tribune's quick action, they then seek to have Paul condemned to death by the Roman governor.

At the beginning of chapter twenty-four, Luke describes how the high priest, Ananias, and a number of elders personally traveled to Caesarea to press the case against Paul. An additional note in Luke's narrative at this point is that Ananias and the elders brought along an orator named Tertullus to serve as their official speaker in denouncing Paul to the governor (24:1).

As Luke reports the outcome of this episode, the pressure generated by Ananias/Tertullus was intense enough to persuade Felix to keep Paul in custody and to keep him from being released two years later when Felix's time in office ended. Luke indicates both of these points as follows: "But when two years had elapsed, Felix was succeeded by Porcius Festus; and desiring to do the Jews a favor, Felix left Paul in prison" (24:27).[20]

Luke next shows that, once the new governor, Festus, had arrived, the chief priest and their allies wasted no time in moving forward against Paul. At the time of the governor's first visit to Jerusalem, they immediately made their allegations against Paul and asked that he be remanded to Jerusalem. Luke does not report that they took this step out of any desire to bring Paul before the Sanhedrin; again he does not portray them as having any judicial interest at this point. Rather he portrays them as "planning an ambush to kill them on the way" (25:3).

What was previously not completely explicit from Luke's earlier reports concerning the character of the chief priest's opposition to Paul is now manifestly clear: they so desire Paul's death that they are prepared to intervene against him themselves.

Prevented from carrying out their plan by Festus' reply that he would conduct an investigation into Paul's case in Caesarea (25:4), the chief priests then revert back to their plan for having Paul executed by judicial verdict. Luke first portrays Festus extending an invitation: "So ... let the men of authority among you go down with me, and if there is anything wrong about the man, let them accuse him" (25:5). Luke then reports the following regarding developments at Caesarea: "the Jews who had gone down from Jerusalem stood about him (Paul), bringing against him many serious charges which they could not prove" (25:7).

Luke next portrays Paul making a direct denial of the charges against him (25:8) and Festus rather quickly bringing forward a proposal of his own. The proposal, inimical to Paul, was that the trial now be shifted back to Jerusalem (25:9).

Using words similar to those he used in describing Felix's motivation for leaving Paul in prison, Luke reports that Festus' reason for wanting to shift Paul's trial back to Jerusalem was that he wished "to do the Jews a favor" (25:9). By the use of this phrase, Luke indicates that the chief priests and their allies had ultimately been successful in influencing Festus to adopt their point of view.

Having delivered this final attack against Paul, and having forced him into a risk-filled appeal to Caesar, the chief priests and their allies then depart from Luke's stage. Paul was once their trusted ally. As a consequence of his conversion, they have come to view him as a dangerous enemy. They themselves were not able to destroy Paul; but by reason of their influence upon Festus they succeeded in leaving him a legacy of continued imprisonment and perhaps ultimately of death.

5. Concluding Reflections

As mentioned at the outset of this study, an analysis of the various forms of opposition that Paul experienced leads to a heightened appreciation of the arduousness of the ministry he conducted. The preceding investigations have highlighted and illuminated the opposition that Paul endured from Jews who refused to accept his message and the opposition that he endured from his former allies, the chief priests of Jerusalem. Similarly, the preceding investigations have also demonstrated that Paul experienced and endured heated opposition from various Gentile groups. What is more, the foregoing analysis has prepared the way for the hypothesis that Luke does not portray Paul as a figure whose commitments and activities are compatible with the Roman social order. Such a hypothesis begins to take shape when Luke's reports about the controversy and opposition stirred by Paul's ministry are viewed from the standpoint of an empire concerned with maintaining peace and order in its provincial system.

In concentrating upon the subject of Paul's non-Roman opponents, the preceding sections have not systematically considered the passages in Acts that describe Paul's interactions with various Roman military and administrative officers.

Under what circumstances does he come before these officials? How does he comport himself in the various proceedings? What is his attitude toward his own Roman citizenship? To whom does he give unqualified allegiance? These and related questions would have to be thematically addressed before any hypothesis regarding Paul's lack of compatibility with the Roman social order could be adequately evaluated.

Nevertheless, significant for the issue of compatibility is the fact that Luke does show Paul experiencing tumultuous and widespread opposition. In several cases this opposition manifested itself in public rioting. And far from intimating that negative reactions to Paul were confined to Jerusalem and Judaea, Luke delineates controversy and opposition in cities and territories throughout the eastern provinces, even locating it in strictly Gentile settings. Read from the vantage point of Roman officials concerned with maintaining provincial order, reports about such a controversy-engendering person assume altogether new dimensions of meaning.

Endnotes

Preface

[1] *The Theology of St. Luke* (London: Faber and Faber, 1960).

[2] *The Acts of the Apostles: A Commentary* (Philadelphia: Westminster, 1971).

[3] *The Making of Luke-Acts* (NY: Macmillan, 1927) and contributions in *The Beginnings of Christianity*, F.J. Foakes Jackson & K. Lake, eds. 5 vols (London: Macmillan, 1920-33).

[4] *Studies in the Acts of the Apostles* (NY: Scribner's, 1956; collection of earlier essays).

[5] W.G. Kummel, "Luc en accusation dans la théologie contemporaine," 93-109 in F. Neirynck, ed., *L'Evangile de Luc: problèmes littéraires et theologiques* (Gembloux: Duculot, 1973—also in *Andover Newton Quarterly* 16 [1975] 131-45); see also W.C. van Unnik, "Luke-Acts: A Storm Center in Contemporary Scholarship," 15-32 in L.E. Keck & J.L. Martyrn eds. *Studies in Luke-Acts* (Nashville: Abingdon, 1966).

[6] F. Bovon, *Luc le theologien: vingt-cinq ans de recherches (1950-1975)* (Neuchâtel: Delachaux & Niestlé, 1978) now see English translation: *Luke the Theologian: Thirty-three Years of Research (1950-1983)* (Princeton Theological Monograph Series 12; Allison Park, Pickwick, 1987); E. Richard, "Luke—Writer, Theologian, Historian: Research and Orientation of the 1970s," *BTB* 13 (1983) 3-15; E. Plümacher, "Acta-Forschung 1974-1982," *TRu* 48 (1983) 1-56 and 49 (1984) 105-69.

Chapter 1

[1] "How to Write History," 34; see A.M. Harmon and K. Kilburn, *Lucian* (Cambridge: Harvard University, 1959-62) 6:2-73.

[2] H.J. Cadbury, "Four Features of Lucan Style," 87-102 in L.E. Keck and J.L. Martyn, eds. *Studies in Luke-Acts* (Nashville: Abingdon, 1966).

[3] See BDF 384-86, 423, 339, 321; also B.M. Metzger, "The Language of the New Testament," in *JB* 7:43-59.

[4] H.J. Cadbury, *The Style and Literary Method of Luke* (Cambridge: Harvard University, 1920) idem. *The Making of Luke-Acts* (NY: Macmillan, 1958); M. Dibelius, *Studies in the Acts of the Apostles* (London: SCM, 1956); G. Schneider, *Das Evangelium nach Lukas* (Gütersloh: Mohn, 1977); and J.A. Fitzmyer, *The Gospel according to Luke* (Garden City: Doubleday, 1981 & 1985).

[5] See E. Richard, "The Old Testament in Acts: Wilcox' Semitisms in Retrospect," *CBQ* 42 (1980) 330-41, for a discussion of alleged translation of Semitic sources.

[6] V.K. Robbins, "Prefaces in Greco-Roman Biography and Luke-Acts," *PRS* 6 (1979) 94-108 and R.J. Dillon, "Previewing Luke's Project from the Prologue (Luke 1:1-4)," *CBQ* 43 (1981) 205-27.

[7] E. Richard, "The Divine Purpose: The Jews and the Gentile Mission (Acts 15)," 188-209 in C.H. Talbert, ed., *Luke-Acts: New Perspectives from the Society of Biblical Literature Seminar* (NY: Crossroad, 1984).

⁸M. Dömer, *Das Heil Gottes: Studien zur Theologie des luchanischen Doppelwerkes* (Cologne: Hanstein, 1978) 160-73.

⁹A. George, "Le sens de la mort de Jésus," 185-212 in *Etudes sur l'oeuvre de Luc* (Paris: Gabalda, 1978); J. Kodell, "Luke's Theology of the Death of Jesus," 221-30 in D. Durken, ed., *Sin, Salvation, and the Spirit* (Collegeville: Liturgical, 1979); and R.L. Brawley, "Paul in Acts: Lucan Apology and Conciliation," 129-47 in Talbert, *Luke-Acts.*

¹⁰The term translated "innocent" at Luke 23:44 is more properly rendered "righteous"; see D. Schmidt, "Luke's 'Innocent' Jesus: A Scriptural Apologetic," 111-21 in R.J. Cassidy and P.J. Scharper, eds. *Political Issues in Luke-Acts* (Maryknoll: Orbis, 1983); and R.J. Karris, *Luke: Artist and Theologian: Luke's Passion Account as Literature* (NY: Paulist, 1985) 95-113.

¹¹See C.H. Talbert, *What Is a Gospel? The Genre of the Canonical Gospels* (Philadelphia: Fortress, 1977); E. Richard, "Luke—Writer, Theologian, Historian: Research and Orientation of the 1970s" *BTB* 13 (1983) 10-12 and idem, *Jesus: One and Many. The Christological Concept of New Testament Authors* (Wilmington, Glazier, 1988) 99-102.

¹²C.H. Talbert, "Prophecies of Future Greatness: The Contribution of Greco-Roman Biographies to an Understanding of Luke 1:5-4:15," 129-41 in J.L. Crenshaw and S. Sandmel, eds. *The Divine Helmsman: Studies on God's Control of Human Events* (NY: Ktav, 1980); see also Fitzmyer, *Luke,* 1:192-219.

¹³W. Kurz, "Luke 22:14-38 and Greco-Roman and Biblical Farewell Addresses," *JBL* 104 (1985) 251-68; M.L. Soards, *The Passion according to Luke: The Special Material of Luke 22* (Sheffield: JSOT, 1987) 21-57, 130-44; and E.S. Steele, "Luke 11:37-54—A Modified Hellenistic Symposium?" *JBL* 103 (1984) 394.

¹⁴P.J. Achtemeier, "The Lukan Perspective on the Miracles of Jesus: A Preliminary Sketch," 153-67 in C.H. Talbert, ed., *Perspectives on Luke-Acts* (Danville: ABPR, 1978).

¹⁵On Lukan sources, see Fitzmyer, *Luke,* 1:63-106.

¹⁶For further discussion, see E. Richard, *Acts 6:1-8:4: The Author's Method of Composition* (Missoula: Scholars, 1978) 254-311 and W.C. van Unnik, "Luke's Second Book and the Rules of Hellenistic HIstoriography," 37-60 in J. Kremer, ed., *Les Actes des Apôtres: tradition, rédaction, théologie* (Gembloux: Duculot, 1979).

¹⁷S.M. Prader, "Acts 27:1-28:16: Sea Voyages in Ancient Literature and the Theology of Luke-Acts," *CBQ* 46 (1984) 683-706.

¹⁸See Lucian, "How to Write History," 33-63.

¹⁹J.A. Fitzmyer, "The Priority of Mark and the 'Q' Source in Luke," 3-40 in *To Advance the Gospel: New Testament Studies* (NY: Crossroad, 1981).

²⁰J.A. Fitzmyer, "The Composition of Luke, Chapter 9," 135-52 in Talbert, *Perspectives.*

²¹Schmidt, "Luke's 'Innocent' Jesus," 11-21.

²²P. Rolland, "L'organization du Livre des Actes et l'ensemble de l'oeuvre de Luc," *Bib* 65 (1984) 81-86.

²³Richard, "Divine Purpose," 188-209.

²⁴J. Dupont, *The Sources of the Acts* (NY: Herder & Herder, 1964).

²⁵M.C. de Boer, "Images of Paul int he Post-Apostolic Period," *CBQ* 42 (1980) 359-80 and Richard, "Luke," 6-8.

[26]V.K. Robbins, "By Land and by Sea: The We-Passages and Ancient Sea Voyages," 215-42 in Talbert, *Perspectives*; one need not agree with the author's literary conclusions to appreciate the evidence and its importance.

[27]J. Kodell, "Luke's Gospel in a Nutshell (Lk 4:16-20)," *BTB* 13 (1983) 16-18.

[28]This expression describes Jesus' role in Acts, where his departure and position at God's side are contrasted with his direct or indirect activity.

[29]W.C. van Unnik, "The 'Book of Acts,' the Confirmation of the Gospel," *NovT* 4 (1960) 26-59; F. Bovon, "L'importance des médiations dans le projet théologique de Luc," *NTS* 21 (1974) 23-39; R.F. O'Toole, "Activity of the Risen Jesus in Luke-Acts," *Bib* 62 (1981) 71-98.

[30]H. Conzelmann, *The Theology of St. Luke* (London: Faber and Faber, 1960); see Richard, "Luke," 3-15 and C.H. Talbert, "Shifting Sands: The Recent Study of the Gospel of Luke," *Int* 30 (1976) 381-95.

[31]Richard, "Luke," 6.

[32]Cadbury, *The Making of Luke-Acts*, 8-9.

[33]See Fitzmyer, *Luke*, 1:311 and R.E. Brown, *The Birth of the Messiah: A Commentary on the Infancy Narratives in Matthew and Luke* (Garden City: Doubleday, 1977) 242-43.

[34]See H.J. Cadbury, *The Book of Acts in History* (NY: Harper, 1955).

[35]D.L. Jones, "The Title *KYRIOS* in Luke-Acts," 96 in *SBL Seminar Papers* (Missoula: Scholars, 1974).

[36]Idem, "The Title *Christos* in Luke-Acts," *CBQ* 32 (1970) 76; also "The Title 'Servant' in Luke-Acts," 146-65 in Talbert, *Luke-Acts*.

[37]Richard, "Divine Purpose," 192-97.

[38]W. Grundmann, "*dei*," *TDNT* 2:22-4; see also Richard, "Divine Purpose," 192-94 and S. Schulz, "Gottes Vorsehung bei Lukas," *ZNW* 54 (1963) 104-16.

[39]D.P. Moessner, "Jesus and the 'Wilderness Generation': The Death of the Prophet Like Moses according to Luke," 319-40 in *SBL Seminar Papers* (Chico: Scholars, 1982).

[40]Richard, "Luke," 9.

[41]E. Richard, "Jesus' Passion and Death in Acts," in D.D. Sylva, ed., *Reimaging the Death of the Lukan Jesus* (Anton Hain: Frankfurt, 1990) 125-52.

[42]R.J. Dillon, "Easter Revelation and Mission Program in Luke 24:46-48," 240-70 in Durken, *Sin, Salvation* and J.-M. Guillaume, *Luc: interprète des anciennes traditions sur la résurrection de Jésus* (Paris: Gabalda, 1979).

[43]E. Richard, "The Creative Use of Amos by the Author of Acts," *NovT* 24 (1982) 51-53.

Chapter 2

[1]For a brief listing and comparison, see J.A. Fitzmyer, *The Gospel according to Luke* (Garden City: Doubleday, 1981 & 1985) 1:288; and for an extended consideration of the parallel ancient texts, see H.J. Cadbury, "Commentary on the Preface of Luke" in F.J. Foakes Jackson and K. Lake, eds., *The Beginnings of Christianity*, Part I: *The Acts of the Apostles* (Grand Rapids: Baker, 1979) 2:489-510.

²Luke's reference to the census under Quirinius is one of the most famous or infamous historical remarks in the NT. There has been a long and still unresolved debate about this information. The many creative attempts to defend the accuracy of Luke's dating are consistently unpersuasive.

³In general, British scholars have tended to defend Luke's dependability as a historian—see, e.g., I.H. Marshall, *Luke: Historian and Theologian* (Grand Rapids: Zondervan, 1970) and German scholars have expressed skepticism about the value of Luke's writings for doing "scientific" history of early Christianity—see, e.g., E. Haenchen, "The Book of Acts as Source Material for the History of Early Christianity" in L.E. Keck and J.L. Martyn, eds. *Studies in Luke-Acts* (London: SPCK, 1968) 258-78. Recently, however, a turn has occurred in the Teutonic tide, for the German scholar M. Hengel, *Acts and the History of Earliest Christianity* (London: SCM, 1979), has defended the veracity of Luke's work in a more thoroughgoing manner than had previous German critics; but Hengel's work itself has not gone without serious negative criticism.

⁴H.J. Cadbury, *The Book of Acts in History* (NY: Harper & Brothers, 1955), offered an extensive, stimulating study of Acts along this line.

⁵I am dependent upon the various standard histories for much of what follows, esp. F.F. Bruce, *New Testament History* (Garden City: Doubleday, 1969); W. Foerster, *From the Exile to Christ* (Philadelphia: Fortress, 1964); J.H. Hayes and J.M. Miller, eds. *Israelites and Judaean History* (Philadelphia: Westminster, 1977); E. Lohse, *The New Testament Environment* (Nashville: Abingdon, 1976); and B. Reicke, *The New Testament Era: The World of the Bible from 500 B.C. to A.D. 100* (Philadelphia: Fortress, 1968).

⁶See esp. F.E. Peters, *The Harvest of Hellenism: A History of the Near East from Alexander the Great to the Triumph of Christianity* (NY: Simon and Schuster, 1970).

⁷Cadbury, *Acts*, 32-57.

⁸*Five Stages of Greek Religion* (Boston: Beacon, 1951).

⁹The difficulty of estimating ancient population is a well-known problem regularly discussed by historians. In what I present here I am using the most conservative estimates. In part, the figures related to the Jewish sects are taken from Josephus, B.J. 2:8:2-14 ## 119-66; Ant. 13:5:9 ## 171-73; 18:1:2-5 ## 11-22.

¹⁰Josephus, Ant. 18:1:3 # 15.

¹¹W.D. Davies, "Contemporary Jewish Religion" in *PCB*, M. Black, ed., (London: Nelson, 1962) 705-11, esp. 706-8, refers to the "assumptions" of the Jewish religion of Jesus' day as "(1) The One God: Monotheism," "(2) His People: Nationalism," and "(3) His Law: Nomism." In this section I modify Davies' terminology slightly and add a forth characteristic to his list. This fourth element of first-century Judaism is the one that many scholars would deny was a part of the everyday religion of "regular" Jews; but a careful examination of the beliefs of first-century Jews as they are reflected in the literature that survives from the period (as that is reflected in later rabbinic memory) shows that *most* (admittedly perhaps not all) first-century Jews had an apocalyptic perspective on the world. This is, however, a highly debated point.

¹²Fitzmyer, *Luke*, 1:400.

¹³A.N. Sherwin-White, *Roman Society and Law in the New Testament* (Oxford: Clarendon, 1963) 11-12, 98.

¹⁴The centurion declares Jesus *dikaios*. Arguments such as those of Fitzmyer, *Luke*, 2:1520, about the meaning of the word on the lips of the historical centurion are surprising, for most critics, including Fitzmyer, consider Luke to be working out of

theological rather than purely historical concerns. A far better understanding of the declaration is to take it as does F.J. Matera, "The Death of Jesus according to Luke," *CBQ* 47 (1985) 469-85, as a theological statement of Jesus' "righteousness." What the centurion knew or could have known is not really the issue for correct interpretation.

[15]See Fitzmyer, *Luke*, 1:651.

[16]Recently A.T. Kraabel, "The Disappearance of the 'God-fearers,'" *Numen* 28 (1981) 113-26 and "The Roman Diaspora: Six Questionable Assumptions," *JJS* 32 (1982) 445-64, has questioned whether "God-fearers" even existed. But, in a general debate conducted between Kraabel and several critics at the annual meeting of the Society of Biblical Literature for 1986 in Atlanta, GA, Kraabel's denial of the existence of "God-fearers" was found incorrect, or at least ill-conceived, though he basically still maintains his position.

[17]See Josephus, B.J. 5, 6, & 7.

[18]C.H. Dodd, "The Fall of Jerusalem and the 'Abomination of Desolation,'" *JRS* 37 (1947) 47-54.

[19]Fitzmyer, *Luke*, 2:1343, delineates exact points of comparison between Luke and Josephus.

[20]See J. Munck, "Discours d'adieu dans le Nouveau Testament et dans la littérature biblique" in *Aux sources de la tradition chrétienne* (Neuchâtel: Delachaux & Niestlé, 1950) 155-70; E. Stauffer, "Abschiedsreden," *RAC* 1 (1950) cols. 29-35; H. Schürmann, *Jesu Abschiedsrede Lk 22, 21-38* (Munster: Aschendorff, 1956) 1-2; R. Schnackenburg, "Abschiedsreden Jesu," *LTK* 1 (1957) cols. 68-69; R.E. Brown, *The Gospel according to John* (Garden City: Doubleday, 1964 & 1970) 2:595-603; G.J. Bahr, "The Seder of the Passover and the Eucharistic Words," *NovT* 12 (1970) 181-202; R. Pesch, *Wie Jesus das Abendmahl hielt: der Grund der Eucharistie* (Freiburg: Herder, 1977) 39; X. Léon-Dufour, "Das lezte Mahl Jesus und die testamentarische Tradition nach Lk 22," *ZKT* 103 (1981) 33-35; T. Huser, Les récits de l'institution de la cène: dissemblances et tradition," *Hokhma* 21 (1982) 28-50.

[21]The classical paradigm is the dialogue of Socrates with his students in Plato's Phaedo. M. Coffey, "Symposium Literature ," in *OCD*, 1028-29, lists works by Xenophon, Aristotle, Epicurus, Maecenas, and Plutarch along with that of Plato. He suggests that "the genre was used . . . as a vehicle for miscellaneous learning and lore" (1028).

[22]See Gen 47:29-50:14; Deuteronomy, esp. chaps.. 32-33; 1 Sam 12:20-25; 1 Kgs 2; and 1 Chr 28-29.

[23]See 1 Macc 2:49-70; 2 Macc 6:30; 7:1-42; 4 Macc; and Tob 4; 14.

[24]See 2 Apoc. Bar. 77:1-26; Test. 12 Patr.; 1 Enoch 91-92; 94-105; Test. of Job; Test. of Moses; 4 Ezra 14:18-50; Test. of Abraham; Test. of Isaac; Test. of solomon; Test. of Jacob; Test. of Adam. J.H. Charlesworth, *The Old Testament Pseudepigrapha* (Garden City: Doubleday, 1983) 1:773, suggests that Test. of Hezekiah (in Martyrdom and Ascension of Isaiah 3:13-4:18), Test. of Zosimus, and Test. of Orpheus should also be consulted in this connection.

[25]See John 13-16; Acts 20:17-38; 1 Tim 4:1; 2 Tim 3:1-4:18; and 2 Pet 1:12-15.

[26]See The Epistle of the Apostles; the Martyrdom of Peter 7-10; and Acts of Andrew 15-18.

[27]See Charlesworth, *Old Testament Pseudepigrapha*, 1:773.

[28]See Léon-Dufour, "Das lezte Mahl Jesu," who argues that 22:1-38 generally conforms to the pattern of final testaments in Test. of 12 Patriarchs. He suggests that

the general form is (a) past, (b) present, and (c) future. Yet, he argues that the most specific parallels can be found between vv. 1-38 and Test. of Naphtali. Léon-Dufour develops an elaborate chart of the parallels between these two works (55). Careful study of the parallels does not always support his suggestions. Perhaps the problem is that he tries to match every element of Luke's testament with some information in Test. of Naphtali, because he does not allow for sufficient variety in the literary genre. But, Léon-Dufour does persuasively show that Luke 22:1-38 belongs to the genre of *testaments*. See also W.S. Kurz, "Luke 22:14-38 and Greco-Roman and Biblical Farewell Addresses," *JBL* 104 (1985) 251-68, who argues that in having Jesus speak at length after the meal, Luke shows that he "had enough rhetorical training to recognize and imitate a literary form and genre such as the farewell address"—though he used no "one farewell speech as his exemplar" (252).

[29]Cadbury, *Acts*, 21-23; and E. Haenchen, *The Acts of the Apostles* (Philadelphia: Westminster, 1971) 424-34.

[30]Cadbury, *Acts*, 21-22.

[31]Haenchen, *Acts*, 426, n. 1.

[32]W.A. Meeks, *The First Urban Christians* (New Haven: Yale University, 1983) 23-25.

[33]This feature of Luke's Gospel is regularly noted by commentators, so much so that A. Plummer, *The Gospel according to St. Luke* (Edinburgh: Clark, 1922), referred to the Third Gospel as the "Gospel of Womanhood," 528.

[34]Haenchen, *Acts*, 517.

[35]Haenchen, *Acts*, 517, n. 10.

[36]O. Bauernfeind, *Die Apostelgeschichte* (Leipzig, 1939) 216 —cited by Haenchen, *Acts*, 517.

[37]Haenchen, *Acts*,. 517-18.

[38]One can observe other ancient writers doing exactly the same, e.g., see Lucian of Samosata on the hypocrisy of Cynic philosophers in both his Philosophies for Sale and The Dead Come to Life.

[39]In addition to Plato's Phaedo, see Aristophanes' Clouds; Xenophon's Apologia Socratis, Memorabilis, and Symposium. See the excellent brief article on Socrates in *OCD*, 997-98.

[40]Similarly, as Luke presents the incident, one sees Paul creating dissension in his appearance before the Sanhedrin in Acts 22:30-23:11.

[41]This conclusion leaves aside the important and often debated issue of whether Luke is writing as an eyewitness (and if so in what manner) or is composing his scenes based upon strictly literary information.

Chapter 3

[1]See, e.g., J.A. Fitzmyer, *The Gospel according to Luke* (Garden City: Doubleday, 1981 & 1985) 1:41-47; G.B. Caird, *Saint Luke* (Baltimore: Penguin, 1963) 15; and A. Plummer, *The Gospel According to St. Luke* (Edinburgh: Clark, 1981) xi-xix.

[2]See, e.g., W.F. Albright, "Luke's Ethnic Background," in J. Munck, *The Acts of the Apostles* (Garden City: Doubleday, 1967) 264-67; E.E. Ellis, *The Gospel of Luke*, (Grand Rapids: Eerdmans, 1974) 53; D.L. Tiede, *Prophecy and History in Luke-Acts* (Philadelphia: Fortress, 1980), who believes that Luke is writing in a prophetic way to convert Jews to Christianity.

³See I.H. Marshall, *Luke: Historian and Theologian* (Exeter: Paternoster, 1970) 103-15.

⁴Ultimately, Luke's conception of God differs from both the Jewish and Greek conceptions. See e.g., Marshall, *ibid.*, and K. Rahner, "Theos in the New Testament," in *Theological Investigations* (NY: Seabury, 1974) 1:79-148.

⁵E. Richard, "The Creative Use of Amos by the Author of Acts," *NovT* 24 (1982) 51-52.

⁶For a discussion of Lukan christology, see E. Richard, *Jesus: One and Many. The Christological Concept of New Testament Authors* (Wilmington: Glazier, 1988) 157-86.

⁷This is one of the numerous titles Luke uses to refer to Jesus in his two-volume work. Other titles are: Lord, Messiah/Christ, Son of God, Son of Man, Servant, Son of David, Prophet, King, Leader, Holy One, Righteous One, Judge, Teacher. Because of space limitations, we will be able to refer in detail only to the more important titles.

⁸In the gospel Luke uses the title "Lord" fourteen times for Jesus. Matthew and Mark each use this title only once for Jesus.

⁹Luke uses "Son of God," "Son of the Most High (God)," and "the/my Son" to refer to Jesus' unique relationship with God.

¹⁰For two different views on Luke's use of this title for Jesus, see Fitzmyer, *Luke*, 1:208-11, and J.D. Kingsbury, *Jesus Christ in Matthew, Mark, and Luke* (Philadelphia: Fortress, 1981) 106-10.

¹¹For the extensive parallels between Jesus and Stephen, see R.F. O'Toole, *The Unity of Luke's Theology: An Analysis of Luke-Acts* (Wilmington: Glazier, 1984) 63-67. For a thorough analysis of the Stephen story, see E. Richard, *Acts 6:1-8:4: The Author's Method of Composition* (Missoula: Scholars, 1978).

¹²Luke's obvious dependence on the Isaian servant songs (cf. Luke 2:32; 22:32; Acts 8:32ff.) suggests that he identifies Jesus as the "Servant" of God in Acts 3:13, 26; 4:27, 30. Luke's portrayal of Paul in the role of the servant (Acts 13:46-47; 26:16-18) supports the claim that Luke intends to present Jesus as a model for his followers.

¹³BAGD, 171.

¹⁴Cf. H.J. Cadbury, *The Making of Luke-Acts* (London: SPCK, 1968) 303-6.

¹⁵See W.S. Kurz, "Hellenistic Rhetoric in the Christological Proof of Luke-Acts," *CBQ* 42 (1980) 171-95.

¹⁶*The Theology of St. Luke* (NY: Harper & Row, 1961).

¹⁷*Ibid.*, 95-136.

¹⁸One who would, however, is E. Grässer, "Die Parusieerwartung in der Apostelgeschichte," in *Les Actes des Apôtres: traditions, rédaction, théologie*, ed. J. Kremer (Gembloux: Duculot, 1979) 99-127.

¹⁹Cf., e.g., S.G. Wilson, "Lukan Eschatology" *NTS* 15 (1969-70) 330-47 and A.J. Mattill, *Luke and the Last Things: A Perspective for the Understanding of Lukan Thought* (Dillsboro: Western North Carolina, 1979).

²⁰E.g., C.H. Talbert, "Shifting Sands: The Recent Study of the Gospel of Luke," *Int* 30 (1976) 386-87.

²¹See E. Franklin, *Christ the Lord: A Study in the Purpose and Theology of Luke-Acts* (Philadelphia: Westminster, 1975) 27, who argues that although in Acts references to the end are few in number, they "are enough to show that Luke wrote against the background of such a belief (Acts 3:20; 10:42; 17:31)."

[22]See, e.g., H.H. Oliver, "The Lucan Birth Stories and the Purpose of Luke-Acts," *NTS* 10 (1964) 202-26; W.B. Tatum, "The Epoch of Israel: Luke 1-2 and the Theological Plan of Luke-Acts," *NTS* 13 (1967) 184-95; W. Wink, *John the Baptist in the Gospel Tradition* (London: Cambridge University, 1968) 55; and Fitzmyer, *Luke*, 1:181-87.

[23]See, e.g., Franklin, *Christ the Lord*, 9-47, and R.J. Dillon, *From Eye-Witnesses to Ministers of the Word: Tradition and Composition in Luke 24* (Rome: Biblical Institute, 1978); cf. E.E. Ellis, *Eschatology in Luke* (Philadelphia: Fortress, 1972).

[24]Franklin, *Christ the Lord*, 174.

[25]Dillon, *From Eye-Witnesses*, 154-55.

[26]*Theology of St. Luke*, 230.

[27]*Ibid.*, 201; cf. 197, n. 3. See also E. Käsemann, "Ministry and Community of the New Testament," in *Essays on New Testament Themes* (London: SCM, 1964) 91-94, who argues that Luke has replaced a theology of the cross with a theology of glory.

[28]See, e.g., A. George, "Le sens de la mort de Jésus," in *Etudes sur l'oeuvre de Luc* (Paris: Gabalda, 1978) 201-11 (published originally as "Le sens de la mort de Jésus pour Luc," *RB* 80 [1973] 186-217); R. Glöckner, *Die Verkündigung des Heils beim Evangelisten Lukas* (Mainz: Matthias-Grunewald, 1976) 155-95; and J. Neyrey, *The Passion According to Luke* (NY: Paulist, 1985) 129-92.

[29]See J. Kodell, "Luke's Theology of the Death of Jesus," in *Sin, Salvation, and the Spirit*, ed. D. Durken (Collegeville: Liturgical, 1979) 221-30.

[30]See, e.g., Neyrey, *The Passion According to Luke*, 137-38; N. Flanagan, "The What and How of Salvation in Luke-Acts," in Durken, *Sin, Salvation, and the Spirit*, 212-13; and O'Toole, *Unity*, 23-32.

[31]See C.H. Talbert, *Luke and the Gnostics* (Nashville: Abingdon, 1966) 17-32, who cites J.M. Wilson, *The Origin and Aim of the Acts of the Apostles* (London: MacMillan, 1912) 80 and U. Wilckens, "Kerygma and Evangelium bei Lukas: Beobachtungen zu Act 10:34-43," *ZNW* 49 (1958) 233.

[32]See George, "Israël," in *Etudes*, 87-125 (originally published as "Israël dans l'oeuvre de Luc," *RB* 75 [1968] 481-525).

[33]See S.G. Wilson, "Law and Judaism in Acts," in *SBL Seminar Papers* (Chico: Scholars, 1980) 251-65, and F.D. Weinert, "The Meaning of the Temple in Luke-Acts," *BTB* 11 (1981) 85-89.

[34]O'Toole, *Unity*, 21; cf. 17, 22, 160-61; see also *Acts 26: The Christological Climax of Paul's Defense (Acts 22:1-26:32)* (Rome: Biblical Institute, 1978) 94, 98.

[35]See E. Haenchen, *The Acts of the Apostles* (Philadelphia: Westminster, 1971) 102; cf. G. Lohfink, *Die Sammlung Israels: Eine Untersuchung zur lukanischen Ekklesiologie* (Munich: Kösel, 1975).

[36]S.G. Wilson, *The Gentiles and the Gentile Mission in Luke-Acts*, (NY: Cambridge, 1973) 227. For a different view, see J. Jervell, "The Divided People of God," in *Luke and the People of God* (Minneapolis: Augsburg, 1972) 41-74, who argues that the acceptance of the good news by the Jews, rather than its rejection, forms the basis for the Gentile mission.

[37]E. Richard, "The Divine Purpose: The Jews and the Gentile Mission (Acts 15)," in *Luke-Acts: New Perspectives from the Society of Biblical Literature Seminar*, ed. C.H. Talbert (NY: Crossroad, 1984) 199.

[38]Franklin, *Christ the Lord*, 119-42, and Jervell, "The Divided People of God," 56.

[39]B.J. Bamberger, "Tax Collector," *IDB* 4:522.

[40]See O.J. Baab, "Woman," *IDB* 4:864-67.

[41]See e.g., H. Flender, *St. Luke: Theologian of Redemptive History* (Philadelphia: Fortress, 1967) 9ff. and O'Toole, *Unity*, 118ff.

[42]R. Bultmann, *"pisteuō," TDNT* 6:208.

[43]See E. Richard, "Luke—Writer, Theologian, Historian: Research and Orientation of the 1970s," *BTB* 13 (1983) 6.

[44]J. Kodell, "The Word of God Grew: The Ecclesial Tendency of *logos* in Acts 1:7; 12:24; 19:20," *Biblica* 55 (1974) 513. Cf. Fitzmyer, *Luke* 1:257.

[45]See, e.g., R. Schnackenburg, "Lukas als Zeuge verschiedener Gemeindestrukturen," *BibLeb* 12 (1972) 232-47.

[46]See Kodell, "'The Word of God grew'."

Chapter 4

[1]N. Peterson, *Literary Criticism for New Testament Critics* (Philadelphia: Fortress, 1978) 5.

[2]There are several books dealing with the history of criticism, e.g., E. Krentz, *The Historical-Critical Method* (Philadelphia: Fortress, 1975), and W.G. Kümmel, *The New Testament: The History of the Investigation of Its Problems* (Nashville: Abingdon, 1972).

[3]For example, R.E. Brown addresses some of the problems associated with the historical critical method in *The Critical Meaning of the Bible* (NY: Paulist, 1981); see especially chap. 2, "What the Biblical Word Meant and What It Means," pp. 23-44.

[4]"Form Criticism and Beyond," *JBL* 88 (1969) 1-18.

[5]*Ibid.*, 8.

[6]Two NT works applying Muilenburg's method are: H.D. Betz, *Galatians: A Commentary on Paul's Letter to the Churches in Galatia* (Philadelphia: Fortress, 1979) and A. Vanhoye, *La structure littéraire de l'Épître aux Hébreux* (Paris: Desclée de Brouwer, 1963).

[7]Peterson, *Literary Criticism*, 88-91.

[8]Luke 4:16-30; 20:9-19; Acts 3:1-4:31; 5:12-42; 13:13-52; 18:1-18.

[9]Peterson uses the term "plot device;" see *Literary Criticism*, 83. Another scholar who uses this term is L.T. Johnson, *The Literary Function of Possessions in Luke-Acts* (Missoula: Scholars, 1977). It is Peterson who suggested the idea of Luke's use of patterned pericopes of confrontation and rejection as a plot device.

[10]The two Old Testament examples that Jesus gives are from 1 Kings 17:1-16; 18:1; and 2 Kings 5:1-14. The point of both these stories for Luke's readers is that the mercy of God was given to Gentiles.

[11]J.A. Fitzmyer, *The Gospel According to Luke* (Garden City: Doubleday, 1981 & 1985) in his extensive and comprehensive commentary devotes 16 pages to this passage including a bibliography of more recent articles (539-40). Other well-known commentaries which treat this passage as programmatic include I.H. Marshall, *The Gospel of Luke* (Grand Rapids: Eerdmans, 1978) 177-90; bibliography pp. 180-81; G. Schneider, *Das Evangelium nach Lukas* (Wurzburg: Echter, 1977) 105-11, bibliography p. 106; H. Schürmann, *Das Lukasvengelium I* Freiburg: Herder, 1969), 225-44, bibliog-

raphy, 225. Cf. also important articles such as: H. Anderson, "Broadening Horizons: The Rejection of Nazareth Pericope of Luke 4, v. 16-30 in Light of Recent Critical Trends," *Int* 18 (1964) 259-75; L.C. Crockett, "Luke 4:25-27 and Jewish-Gentile Relations in Luke-Acts," *JBL* 88 (1969) 177-83; D. Hill, "The Rejection of Jesus at Nazareth (Luke IV, 16-30)," *NovT* 13 (1974) 161-80; J.A.Sanders, "From Isaiah 61 to Luke 4," in *Christianity, Judaism and Other Greco-Roman Cults*, ed. J. Neusner (Leiden: Brill, 1975) 75-106; R.C. Tannehill, "The Mission of Jesus According to Luke IV, 16-30," in *Jesus in Nazareth,* ed. E. Grässer et al. (Berlin: de Gruyter, 1972) 51-75.

[12]M. Rodgers, "Luke 4:26-30 —A Call for a Jubilee Year?" *RTR* 40 (1981) 72-82, 81.

[13]In the Markan form of this story (6:1-6), the initial reaction of the people was one of hostility. They were scandalized (*eskandalizonto*) at Jesus. Hence, there was rejection and hostility from the start. Not so in Luke. See Tannehill, "The Mission of Jesus," 51-75.

[14]Anderson, "Broadening Horizons," 259-75, 266.

[15]Crockett, "Luke 4:25-27 and Jewish-Gentile Relations," 177-83, 178.

[16]*Ibid.* These details are given in Elijah traditions contemporary with Luke. Sirach 48, Biblical Antiquities of Pseudo-Philo, and Revelation 11:6 speak of Elijah closing the heavens; James 5:17 uses the three and one-half years tradition.

[17]*Ibid.*

[18]*Ibid.*, 181.

[19]*Ibid.*, 183. Some scholars would disagree with Crockett and see Luke 4:25-27 as signaling the rejection of the Jewish people by Jesus.

[20]Crockett, "Luke 4:25-27 and Jewish-Gentile Relations," 183.

[21]F. Hauch and S.Schultz, "poreuomai," *TDNT*, 6:575.

[22]Acts 28:30-31 does not mention Jews specifically, but the context suggests that at least some of those who came to him would be Jews. Cf. Acts 28:23.

[23]E. Richard, in his article "The Divine Purpose: The Jews and the Gentile Mission (Acts 15)" in *Luke-Acts: New Perspectives from the Society of Biblical Literature Seminar*, ed. C.H. Talbert (NY: Crossroad, 1984),188-209, notes that rejection episodes can serve different functions in the narrative of Acts; cf. n. 52, p. 207.

[24]Refer back to the analysis of Luke 4:16-30.

Chapter 5

[1]For references to the wide-ranging discussion concerning genre, see C.A. Evans, "The Hermeneutics of Mark and John: On the Theology of the Canonical Gospels," *Bib* 64 (1983) 153-72, esp. 153-55.

[2]C.H. Talbert, *What is a Gospel? The Genre of the Synoptic Gospels* (Philadelphia: Fortress, 1977) and D.L. Barr and J.L. Wentling, "The Conventions of Classical Biography and the Genre of Luke-Acts: A Preliminary Story," 63-88, esp. 76, in *Luke-Acts: New Perspectives from the Society of Biblical Literature*, ed. C.H. Talbert (NY: Crossroad, 1984).

[3]"The Conventions of Classical Biography," 76.

[4]R.E. Brown, "Jesus and Elisha," *Perspective* 12 (1971) 85-104; M. Hengel, *Acts and the History of Earliest Christianity* (Philadelphia: Fortress, 1980) 3-39, esp. 31.

⁵See A. Wiener, *The Prophet Elijah in the Development of Judaism: a Depth-Psychological Study* (Boston: Routledge & Kegan Paul, 1978); M.J. Stiassny, "Le Prophète Elie dans le Judaïsme," 199-255 in *Elie le prophète, II* (Paris: Desclée de Brouwer, 1956) 199-255.

⁶Wiener, *The Prophet Elijah*, 174-98.

⁷See J.L. Martyn, *The Gospel of John in Christian History* (NY: Paulist, 1978) 9-54.

⁸For opinions, see L. Bonner, *The Stories of Elijah and Elisha* (Lieden: Brill, 1968) 30-34; G. Hentschel, *Die Elijaerzahlungen* (Leipzig: St. Benno, 1977) 1-9.

⁹For contrasting views of how this relationship may have originated, see P. Ellis ("1-2 Kings," in *JBC* 1:194) and R. Kilian, "Die Totenerweckungen Elias und Elisas eine Motivwanderung," *BZ* 10 (1966) 44-56.

¹⁰See, for instance, A. Sanda, *Die Bücher der Könige, II* (Munster: Aschendorffsche, 1912) 2.

¹¹See T.L. Brodie, "Greco-Roman Imitation of Texts as a Partial Guide to Luke's Use of Sources," 17-46 in Talbert, *Luke-Acts; New Perspectives*.

¹²See, for instance, D.L. Tiede, *Prophecy and History in Luke-Acts* (Philadelphia: Fortress, 1980) 19-55; L.T. Johnson, *The Literary Function of Possession in Luke-Acts* (Missoula: Scholars, 1977) 91-96.

¹³J.A. Fitzmyer, *The Gospel According to Luke* (Garden City: Doubleday, 1981 & 1985) 1:214.

¹⁴*Ibid.*, 213-15.

¹⁵See J.A.T. Robinson, "Elijah, John and Jesus: an Essay in Detection," *NTS* 4 (1958) 263-81.

¹⁶See by T.L. Brodie, "Towards Unraveling Luke's Use of the Old Testament: Luke 7:11-17 as an *Imitation* of 1 Kings 17:17-24," *NTS* 32 (1986) 247-67; "Luke 7:36-50 as an Internalization of 2 Kings 4:1-37: a Study in Luke's Use of Rhetorical Imitation," *Bib* 64 (1983) 457-85; "The Departure for Jerusalem (Luke 9:51-56) as a Rhetorical Imitation of Elijah's Departure for the Jordan (2 Kings 1:1-2:6)," *Bib* 70 (1989) 96-109; "The Accusing and Stoning of Naboth (1 Kings 21:8-13) as One Component of the Stephen Text (Acts 6:9-14; 7:58a)," *CBQ* 45 (1983) 417-32; "Toward Unraveling the Rhetorical Imitation of Sources in Acts 2 Kings 5 as One Component of Acts 8, 9-40," *Bib* 67 (1986) 41-67.

¹⁷Cf. idem, *Luke the Literary Interpreter: Luke-Acts as a Systematic Rewriting and Updating of the Elijah-Elisha Narrative* (Rome: Angelicum University, 1987) 134-253, 272-366 (available through Univ. Microf. Intern., publication no. 88-10, 615).

¹⁸For a survey of the *literary* balance, see C.H. Talbert, *Literary Patterns, Theological Themes and the Genre of Luke-Acts* (Missoula: Scholars, 1974) 15-23. Even if one does not accept all of Talbert's alleged parallels, he and those whose work he is summarizing are clearly dealing with some form of correspondence between the two parts of Luke-Acts.

¹⁹R.J. Dillon, *From Eye-witnesses to Ministers of the Word* (Rome: Biblical Pontifical Institute, 1978) 177-78.

²⁰G. Lohfink, *Die Himmelfahrt Jesu* (Munich: Kösel, 1971) 79.

²¹R. Pesch, "Der Anfang der Apostelgeschichte: Apg. 1, 1-11. Kommentarstudie," *EKKNT Vorarb* (Zurich: Benziger, 1971) 3:7-36, esp. 15-17, gives a clear account of the verbal similarities surrounding the assumption/ascension texts but is unsure whether the relationship is literary. Thus, Pesch comes close to indicating a direct

literary connection, but because he does not see the data in context —within the broad context of the general practice of imitation, and within the more immediate context of Luke's affinity with aspects of the Elijah-Elisha narrative —he reaches a conclusion which is fairly accurate but which needs greater refinement and conclusiveness.

²²Brodie, "The Accusing of Naboth," 421-22.

²³For a more detailed analysis of the similarities between the two assumption/ ascension accounts, see Brodie, *Luke the Literary Interpreter*, 254-69.

²⁴See Talbert, *What is a Gospel*, 95-96, 134; Barr and Wentling, "The Genre of Luke-Acts," 73-74.

Chapter 6

¹F.C.Burkitt, *The Gospel History and Its Transmission* (Edinburgh: Clark, 1906) 135; R. Bultmann, *The History of the Synoptic Tradition* (NY: Harper & Row, 1963-German original 1921) 362; W.G. Kümmel, *Introduction to the New Testament* (Nashville: Abingdon, 1975—German original 1973) 130-31; and F. Neirynck, "The Argument From Order and St. Luke's Transpositions," *ETL* 49 (1973) 784-815.

A modified form of the two-document hypotesis (i.e., Mark and Q plus L and M) is the solution to the so-called Synoptic problem that informs this study of Luke 22:63-65. This way of understanding the relationship of the Synoptic gospels to one another has not gone without criticism from scholars like W.R. Farmer, a vigorous opponent of either the two-document or modified two-document hypothesis and an energetic advocate of the Griesbach hypothesis that Mark is an abridgment of Matthew and Luke. Farmer's position, as representative of those defending the validity of the Griesbach hypothesis, may be seen in his book, *The Synoptic Problem: A Critical Analysis* (Dillsboro: Western North Carolina, 1976) or his article, "A 'Skeleton in the Closet' of Gospel Research," *BR* 9 (1961) 18-42. Some of the most recent investigations related to the questions comprising the Synoptic problem are found in *New Synoptic Studies: The Cambridge Gospel Conference and Beyond*, ed. W.R. Farmer (Macon: Mercer University, 1983).

Kümmel offers a thorough survey of the Synoptic problem and the various solutions that have been offered to it in *Introduction*, 38-80. For the purpose of the present study, a careful and persuasive espousal of the legitimacy of the modified two-document hypothesis for the study of Luke is J.A. Fitzmyer's article, "The Priority of Mark and the 'Q' Source in Luke," *Perspectives* 11 (1970 —also entitled *Jesus and Man's Hope*) 1:131-70; reprinted in *To Advance the Gospel: New Testament Studies* (NY: Crossroad, 1981) 3-40.

²In general the distinction between "composition" and "redaction" is clearly described by J.A. Fitzmyer, *The Gospel according to Luke* (Garden City: Doubleday, 1981 & 1985) 1:85, who defines *composition* as "verses (Luke) wrote to present the story about Jesus and the sequel thereto in the form that he was interested in" and *redaction* as "the editorial modifications of source-material that Luke had taken over."

Often various authors will judge that in one place Luke is freely composing while in another place Luke is redacting tradition. For example, Bultmann, *History*, 282-83, claims that the healing of the ear cut off from the servant of the high priest (2:51) "goes back to Luke himself." Yet, for the Lukan account of the last supper, esp. 22:14-18, Bultmann (279) claims that Luke "has another and indeed older report than Mark." Bultmann even suggests that here Luke draws upon a special source that was written.

³This line of thought is represented in G. Schneider's statement that "if one takes into account the continuation of oral tradition both at the time of and following the

composition of the gospels, then one needs to postulate no connected special source for the special material of the third evangelist," *Das Evangelium nach Lukas* (Gütersloh: Mohn, 1977) 2:436.

[4]The history of this position is admirably surveyed by V. Taylor, *The Passion Narrative of St. Luke* (NY: Cambridge University, 1972) 3-27. Since Taylor's work appeared in 1972, J. Ernst, *Das Evangelium nach Lukas* (Regensberg: Pustet, 1977) esp. 643-44, has taken this position. In 1982, E. Schweizer (who admits that the question about a special source cannot be finally answered) made a case for a special source, *Das Evangelium nach Lukas* (Göttingen: Vandenhoeck & Ruprecht, 1982) 235-36. Schweizer's position is generally consistent with his earlier argument for a "Hebraizing" source in Luke; see "Eine hebraisierende Sonderquelle des Lukas?" *TZ* 6 (1950) 161-85.

[5]See R. Scroggs, "Section IV: Markan Stylistic Characteristics in Introductory and Concluding Phrases and Sentences" in W. Kelber, A. Kolenkow, and R. Scroggs, "Reflections on the Question: Was There a Pre-Markan Passion Narrative?" *SBL Seminar Papers* (Missoula: Scholars, 1971) 503-85, esp. 529.37.

[6]This judgment is shared by R.E. Brown, *The Birth of the Messiah* (Garden City: Doubleday, 1977) 246 and is recognized even in the editorial comments of O.E. Evans in Taylor's *Passion* (27-39).

[7]I deliberately refer to the accounts of Jesus' appearance before the Jewish council in Mark and Luke using different words: "trial" for Mark and "examination" for Luke. Clearly Mark portrays Jesus as facing formal legal charges in a formal (though jaundiced) legal process. Luke narrates the story so that Jesus' appearance before the council is more a preliminary hearing, something like a modern grand jury probe of allegations that seeks to determine whether sufficient evidence of wrongdoing exists to warrant a trial.

[8]Scholars have completely different opinions about the relationship. J. Finegan, *Die Überlieferung der Leidens-und Auferstehungsgeschichte Jesu* (Giessen: Töpelmann, 1934) 24, simply equates these portions of Mark and Luke. A.M. Perry, *The Sources of Luke's Passion-Narrative* (Chicago: University, 1920) 44, admits that the idea portrayed in 22:63-65 is similar to that in Mark 14:65 *but* he maintains that Luke's scene "contains no materials closely resembling Mark, and its general agreement is but 18 per cent; so it may be ascribed entirely to J [i.e., Perry's symbol for Luke's special non-Markan source]." In four places, Schneider argues that the "scoffing" of Jesus in Luke is without Markan parallel. He concludes, vv. 63-65 are from a source additional to Mark, although Luke incorporated the Markan command, "Prophesy," into that source; see *Verleugnung, Verspottung und Verhor Jesu nach Lukas 22, 54-71: Studien zur lukanischen Darstellung der Passion* (Munich: Kösel, 1969) 97-104, 137-39; "Das Problem einer vorkanonischen Passionserzahlung," *BZ* 16 (1972) 236; *Die Passion Jesu nach der drei ateren Evangelien* (Munich: Kösel, 1973) 68-69; and *Evangelium*, 2:437, 464-65.

[9]Of course, Mark 15:16-20 is another Markan mockery scene, but Luke "omitted" that particular episode, using its narrative actions and adapting its theological motifs in the uniquely Lukan passion incident of Jesus' appearing before Herod Antipas (Luke 23:6-12). See M.L. Soards, "Tradition, Composition, and Theology in Luke's Account of Jesus before Herod Antipas," *Bib* 66 (1985) 344-64.

[10]Above all, see Schneider, *Verleugnung*, passim, esp. 96-104.

[11]See I.H. Marshall, *The Gospel of Luke: A Commentary on the Greek Text* (Grand Rapids: Eerdmans, 1978) 846, who argues that this explanation would account for other non-Markan elements found in Matthew's version of this story.

[12]Compare Schweizer, *Evangelium*, 232, who argues that the exact verbal agreement between Luke 22:62, 64 and Matt 26:75, 68 cannot be accounted for in terms of oral tradition.

Recent studies suggest that Schweizer underestimates the power of memory and the vitality of oral tradition in pre-Gutenberg cultures; see W. Kelber, *The Oral and Written Gospel* (Philadelphia: Fortress, 1983) 13.

[13]Compare Bultmann, *History*, 271, who argues that *tis estin ho paisas se* is "in all probability a wholly secondary conformation to Matthew."

[14]A similar explanation is given by R. Schnackenburg, *The Gospel according to St. John* (NY: Crossroad, 1982) 3:31. But, for a radically different explanation that maintains there was historical and perhaps literary contact between Luke and John, see J.A. Bailey, *The Traditions Common to the Gospels of Luke and John* (Leiden: Brill, 1963).

[15]A strong case may be made for a written source, namely Q, as the explanation of the similarities between Luke 22:28-30 and Matt 19:28.

[16]Compare E. Lohse, *History of the Suffering and Death of Jesus Christ* (Philadelphia: Fortress, 1967) 40, 72, who remarks that while Luke may be dependent upon a tradition other than Mark, it is difficult, if not impossible, to determine exactly *if* and *what* that tradition was.

[17]Schneider, *Evangelium*, 2:465.

[18]Bultmann, *History*, 271; E. Klostermann, *Das Lukasevangelium* (Tübingen: Mohr, 1929) 221; and Finegan, *Überlieferung*, 25.

[19]See, in agreement, Finegan, *Überlieferung*, 24. One of the major objections to the understanding of 22:63-65 articulated here is that in its grammatical context the pronominal object of the mockery (*auton*) refers to Peter, not Jesus; see Marshall, *Commentary*, 846. Two factors overrule this objection: first, Peter is clearly out of the scene; second, no one has been in charge of Peter. Therefore, it is best to understand that Luke thought the phrase *hoi andres hoi synechontes* governing "him" provided sufficient grammatical context for *auton*.

[20]Compare Ernst, *Evangelium*, 616, who claims that it was *guards* who had custody of Jesus prior to the assembly meeting. *Pace* Ernst, from Luke's story, there is no clear change of groups from the arrest to the mockery.

[21]See Schneider, *Evangelium*, 2:464-65; R.J. Karris, *Invitation to Luke* (NY: Doubleday, 1977) 254-55.

[22]D.L. Miller, "*EMPAIZEIN*: Playing the Mock Game (Luke 22:63-64)," *JBL* 90 (1971) 309-13, treats these verses in relation to references to games in ancient literature. He argues that Jesus is the victim in a game, *chalkē muïa*, like "blindman's bluff." While Miller does argue his case persuasively, see his work for the range of possible ancient games that could have been played on this occasion.

[23]This intimidation is related to an "intimidation motif" often found in martyr literature: see Schneider, *Evangelium*, 2:464-65; H. Hendrickx, *The Passion Narratives of the Synoptic Gospels* (Manila: East Asian Pastoral Institute, 1977) 64.

An *intimidation motif* is an established feature of martyr accounts in both Jewish and non-Jewish Hellenistic literature of Luke's day. Schneider, *Evangelium*, 2:464-65, lists 2 Macc 7:1-2, 7, 12; 4 Macc 6:3-30; 8:12-14:10 as examples of the intimidation motif in Jewish literature. S.K. Williams, *Jesus' Death as Saving Event: The Background and Origin of a Concept* (Missoula: Scholars, 1975), attends to these texts and others in Philo, Plato, and Plutarch (see esp. 141-44). Luke employed the motif to reinforce the image of Jesus as being in charge of all that occurs around him.

[24]This exposition of the function of irony in this portion of Luke's passion narrative is indebted to the stimulating treatment of irony in R.A. Culpepper, *Anatomy of the Fourth Gospel: A Study in Literary Design* (Philadelphia: Fortress, 1983) 165-80.

Chapter 7

[1]For recent treatments of Paul's portrait in Acts, with a review of issues raised by the accounts of his Damascus experience; see R.L. Brawley, "Paul in Acts: Aspects of Structure and Characterization," in *SBL Seminar Papers* (Atlanta: Scholars, 1988) 90-105; J.T. Carroll, "Literary and Social Dimensions of Luke's Apology for Paul," *ibid.*, 106-18; J.T. Townsend, "Acts 9:1-29 and Early Church Tradition," *ibid.*, 119-31. See B.R. Gaventa, *From Darkness to Light: Aspects on Conversion in the New Testament* (Philadelphia: Fortress, 1986) and "The Overthrown Enemy: Luke's Portrait of Paul," in *SBL Seminary Papers* (Chico: Scholars, 1985) 439-49.

[2]P. Schubert, "The Final Cycle of Speeches in the Book of Acts," *JBL* 87 (1968) 1-16; F. Veltman, "The Defense Speeches of Paul in Acts," in C.H. Talbert, ed. *Perspectives on Luke-Acts* (Danville: ABPR, 1978) 243-56. For an annotated study of various literary studies, including speeches, present in the New Testament, with the focus on Luke-Acts, see D.E. Aune, *The New Testament in Its Literary Environment* (Philadelphia: Westminster, 1987); see his comment: "In Luke-Acts, speeches are an essential feature of the action itself, which is the spread of the word of God" (125-26). See J. Neyrey, "The Forensic Defense Speech and Paul's Trial Speeches in Acts 22-26: Form and Function," in C.H. Talbert, ed., *Luke-Acts: New Perspectives from the Society of Biblical Literature Seminary* (NY: Crossroad, 1984) 210-24; P. Walaskay, "*And so We Came to Rome*": *The Political Perspective of St. Luke* (NY: Cambridge University, 1984).

[3]G. Genette, *Narrative Discourse: An Essay in Method* (NY: Cornell University, 1985); first published as *Discours du récit* (Paris: Editions du Seuil, 1972). Genette's discussion of terms is divided under five headings: order, duration, frequency, mood, and voice.

[4]More exactly, immediate and mimetic narration are sub-categories of "distance" which indicates how close or removed a speaker is from the actions being narrated; cf., Genette, *Narrative Discourse*, 162-69.

[5]*Ibid.*, 33-85.

[6]See S. Lundgren, "Ananias and the Calling of Paul in Acts," *ST* 25 (1971) 117-22; G. Schneider, *Lukas: Aufsatze zum lukanischen Doppelwerk* (Köningstein: Hanstein, 1985) 627.

[7]See D.P. Moessner, "Paul and the Pattern of the Prophet Like Moses," in *SBL Seminar Papers* (Chico: Scholars, 1983) 203-12, for a description of the accusations against Paul that parallel those brought against Jesus and Stephen.

[8]Paul is called Saul up until the end of the encounter with Elymas and Sergius Paulus on Cyprus, when the magician is struck blind and Sergius Paulus believes the message of Barnabas and Saul (13:4-12). See K. Stendahl, *Paul Among Jews and Gentiles* (Philadelphia: Paulist, 1983) 11, on the reason for the change of name in the passage from "Saul" to "Paul": "This is Paul's first encounter with Roman officials, and if the purpose of Acts is to show the gospel's way from Jerusalem to Rome (cf. Acts 1:8), then it is clear that the name change symbolizes the change of focus. From now on, Rome is the 'magnet.' The mission is in focus—therefore the call, not the conversion."

[9]H.H. Schaeder, "*Nazarenos, Nazoraios*," *TDNT* 4:874-79.

[10]See F.F. Bruce, *Commentary on the Book of Acts* (Grand Rapids: Eerdmans, 1972) 90, for the forms the name of Jesus takes; J.A.Ziesler, "The Name of Jesus in the Acts of the Apostles," *JSNT* 4 (1979) 28-41.

[11]See *ibid.*, 403, for a comparison of the words of Ananias with data in the Pauline epistles.

[12]Cf. O. Betz, "Die Vision des Paulus im Tempel von Jerusalem: Apg 22:17-21 als Beitrag zur Deutung des Damaskuserlebnis," in *Verborum Veritas*, eds. O. Bücher et al (Wuppertal: Brockhaus, 1970) 113-23.

[13]Genette, *Narrative Discourse*, 161-211, discusses the term "mood" by which he means both point of view and narrational perspective.

[14]The interrelation of Luke's narration of the Damascus episode and that of Cornelius' vision in Acts 10-11 is suggested by W.S. Kurz, "The Influence of Variant Narrators on Repeated Acts Narratives," *AAR/SBL Abstracts* (Atlanta: Scholars, 1988) 261. See also Kurz, "Narrative Approaches to Luke-Acts," *Bib* 68 (1987) 195-220.

Chapter 8

[1]For a more thorough presentation of this topic, see D.M. Sweetland, *Our Journey with Jesus: Discipleship according to Luke-Acts* (Collegeville: The Liturgical Press, 1990).

[2]See D.M. Sweetland, *Our Journey with Jesus: Discipleship according to Mark* (Wilmington: Glazier, 1987) 22-23.

[3]See K.N. Giles, "The Church in the Gospel of Luke," *SJT* 34 (1981) 140-41, and S. Brown, *Apostasy and Perseverance in the Theology of Luke* (Rome: Pontifical Biblical Institute, 1969) 56, 82f.

[4]See G.W.H. Lampe, "The Holy Spirit in the Writings of St. Luke," in *Studies in the Gospels*, ed. D.E. Nineham (Oxford: Blackwell, 1957) 159.

[5]The journey situation is mentioned or alluded to in 9:51, 53, 56, 57; 10:1, 38; 13:22, 31, 33, 35; 14:25; 17:11; 18:31, 35, 36; 19:1, 11, 28, 29, 36, 37, 41, 45. Jerusalem is mentioned specifically in 9:51, 53; 13:22, 33; 17:11; 18:31; 19:11, 28 (cf. 19:41, 45).

[6]On the importance of the mission theme see S.G. Wilson, *The Gentiles and the Gentile Mission in Luke-Acts* (NY: Cambridge, 1973); R.J. Dillon, "Easter Revelation and Mission Program in Luke 24:46-48," in D. Durkin, ed., *Sin, Salvation, and the Spirit* (Collegeville: Liturgical, 1979) 240-70; and E. Richard, "The Divine Purpose: The Jews and the Gentile Mission (Acts 15)," in C.H. Talbert, ed., *Luke-Acts: New Perspectives from the Society of Biblical Literature Seminar* (NY: Crossroad, 1984) 188-209.

[7]See C.H. Talbert, *Literary Patterns, Theological Themes and the Genre of Luke-Acts* (Missoula: Scholars, 1974) 95-96; R.F. O'Toole, "Parallels between Jesus and His Disciples in Luke-Acts: A Further Study," *BZ* 27 (1983) 197, and *The Unity of Luke's Theology: An Analysis of Luke-Acts* (Wilmington: Glazier, 1984) 72; and Richard, "The Divine Purpose."

[8]J.A. Fitzmyer, *The Gospel According to Luke* (Garden City: Doubleday, 1981 & 1985) 1:241.

[9]*Ibid.*, 1:235.

[10]Brown, *Apostasy*, 58, n. 213; P.J. Achtemeier, "The Lukan Perspective on the Miracles of Jesus: A Preliminary Sketch," in Talbert, *Perspectives*, 161; and C.H. Talbert, *Reading Luke* (NY: Crossroad, 1984) 59.

[11]Cf. W.C. Robinson, "The Theological Context for Interpreting Luke's Travel Narrative (9:51ff.)," *JBL* 79 (1960) 20-31; C.H. Talbert, *Luke and the Gnostics* (Nashville: Abingdon, 1966) 17-32; J. Navone, *Themes of St. Luke* (Rome: Gregorian, 1970) 199-210; and Fitzmyer, *Luke*, 1:243.

[12]Fitzmyer, *Luke*, 1:569.

[13]Talbert, *Reading*, 63. Cf. E. Best, *Following Jesus: Discipleship in the Gospel of Mark* (Sheffield: JSOT, 1981) 178, who suggests that the call of Levi in Mark be understood in this way.

[14]J. Behm, "*metanoeō*," *TDNT* 4:1002.

[15]See J. Kodell, "'The Word of God grew': The Ecclesial Tendency of *logos* in Acts 1, 7; 12, 24; 19, 20," *Bib* 55 (1974) 514, who follows R. Michiels, "La conception lucanienne de la conversion," *ETL* 41 (1965) 42-78.

[16]M. Dibelius, *Studies in the Acts of the Apostles* (NY: Scribner's, 1956) 165; J. Dupont, "Repentir et conversion d'après les Acts des Apôtres," *ScEccl* 12 (1960) 137-73; and R.J. Karris, *Invitation to Acts* (Garden City: Doubleday, 1978) 40. Cf. also E. Schweizer, "Concerning the Speeches in Acts," in *Studies in Luke-Acts*, eds. L.E. Keck and J.L. Martyn (Nashville: Abingdon, 1966) 208-16, and Navone, *Themes*, 38-46.

[17]See A. Trites, "The Prayer Motif in Luke-Acts," in Talbert, *Perspectives*, 168-86.

[18]H.J. Cadbury, *The Making of Luke-Acts* (London: SPCK, 1968) 269; Fitzmyer, *Luke*, 1:244-47; Talbert, *Reading*, 102-104, 132; and O'Toole, *Unity*, 72.

[19]It is widely recognized that Luke 9:61-62 alludes to 1 Kings 19:19ff. Luke is implicitly drawing attention to the fact that the demands of Jesus are more stringent than those of Elijah.

[20]See e.g., E.E. Ellis, *The Gospel of Luke* (Camden: Nelson, 1966) 152; M. Miyoshi, *Der Anfang des Reiseberichts, Lk 9:51-10:24: Eine redaktionsgeschichtliche Untersuchung* (Rome: Pontifical Biblical Institute, 1974) 74-75; and Fitzmyer, *Luke*, 1:842.

[21]Cadbury, *Making*, 267-68; Navone, *Themes*, 71-87; P.J. Bernadicou, "Christian Community According to Luke," *Worship* 44 (1970) 213ff., and "The Spirituality of Luke's Travel Narrative," *RevRel* 36 (1977) 460-63; and O'Toole, *Unity*, 225-60.

[22]E.g., Luke 5:25-26; 6:20-23; 15:4-32; 19:37-44; 24:50-53.

[23]E.g., Acts 2:26-27, 42-47; 13:48, 52; 15:3, 31.

[24]See Talbert, *Reading*, 173, and Fitzmyer, *Luke*, 2:1205-1206.

[25]Cf. Fitzmyer, *Luke*, 1:223-24 and O'Toole, *Unity*, 51.

[26]R. Bultmann, "*pisteuō*," *TDNT* 6:208.

[27]Fitzmyer, *Luke*, 1:240-41.

[28]See D.B. Kraybill and D.M. Sweetland, "Possessions in Luke-Acts: A Sociological Perspective," *PRS* 10 (1983) 224-27.

[29]See, e.g., R. Schnackenburg, "Lukas als Zeuge verschiedener Gemeindestrukturen," *BibLeb* 12 (1972) 232-47.

[30]D.M. Sweetland, "The Lord's Supper and the Lukan Community," *BTB* 13 (1983) 27. Cf. also J. Wanke, *Beobachtungen zum Eucharistieverständnis des Lukas auf Grund der lukanischen Mahlberichte* (Leipzig: St. Benno, 1973).

[31]Bernadicou, "Community," 205-19; E.A. LaVerdiere and W.G. Thompson, "New Testament Communities in Transition: A Study of Matthew and Luke," *TS* 37 (1976) 591f.; and O'Toole, *Unity*, 255.

³²See W.E. Pilgrim, *Good News to the Poor* (Minneapolis: Augsburg, 1981) 129-34, who regards the Zacchaeus story "as the most important Lukan text on the subject of the right use of possessions." Cf. Fitzmyer, *Luke*, 2:1218-27.

³³Jesus speaks favorably of almsgiving in the Zacchaeus story and in Luke 11:41; 12:33; 16:9; 18:22.

³⁴L.T. Johnson, *The Literary Function of Possessions in Luke-Acts* (Missoula: Scholars, 1977) 127-71.

Chapter 9

¹For studies of God the Father in the Synoptics, see G. Schrenk, "*patēr*," *TDNT* 5:974-96; B.M.F. van Iersel, '*Der Sohn*' *in den synoptischen Jesusworten* (Leiden: Brill, 1961) 93-116; W. Marchel, *Abba, Père! la prière du Christ et des chrétiens* (Rome: Biblical Institute, 1963); J. Jeremias, *The Prayers of Jesus* (Naperville: Allenson, 1967) 11-65; idem, *New Testament Theology* (NY: Scribner's, 1971) 36-37, 56-68; R. Hamerton-Kelly, *God the Father* (Philadelphia: Fortress, 1979). These studies tend to focus on the words of the historical Jesus rather than the emphases of the individual Synoptics.

²J.A. Fitzmyer, *The Gospel According to Luke* (Garden City: Doubleday, 1981 & 1985) 1:443.

³J.D.G. Dunn, *Jesus and the Spirit* (Philadelphia: Westminster, 1975) 32; *contra* Jeremias, *New Testament Theology*, 56-59.

⁴J. Neyrey, *The Passion According to Luke* (NY: Paulist, 1985) 24. Concerning the translation of this verse, see I.H. Marshall, *The Gospel of Luke* (Grand Rapids: Eerdmans, 1978) 817.

⁵This is undoubtedly true if, as B.D. Ehrman and M.A. Plunkett, "The Angel and the Agony: The Textual Problem of Luke 22:43-44," *CBQ* 45 (1983) 401-16, argue 22:43-44 is an interpolation. Yet Neyrey, *The Passion According to Luke*, 62, who defends the authenticity of these verses, also concludes that Jesus' obedience to the will of God is the focus of this unit.

⁶See Marshall, *Luke*, 867-68; Fitzmyer, *Luke*, 2:1503-4.

⁷This verse presumably does not rest on a special Lukan source; cf. Marshall, *Luke*, 874; J. Jeremias, *Die Sprache des Lukasevangeliums* (Göttingen: Vandenhoeck & Ruprecht, 1980) 307-9; Fitzmyer, *Luke*, 2:1513.

⁸R.E. Brown, *The Birth of the Messiah* (Garden City: Doubleday, 1977) 481, argues that "if there was a pre-Lucan story, one must recognize that Luke has thoroughly rewritten it."

⁹E. Bammel, "*Das Ende von Q*," *Verborum Veritas*, eds. O. Böcher et al. (Wuppertal: Brockhaus, 1970) 44-50; J.D. Crossan, *In Fragments: The Aphorisms of Jesus* (San Francisco: Harper & Row, 1983) 204; and Marshall, *Luke*, 815, assume that this verse is from Q material, while H. Schürmann, *Jesu Abschiedsrede: Lk 22, 21-38* (Münster: Aschendorff, 1957) 40-44; and V. Taylor, *The Passion Narrative of St. Luke* (London: Cambridge University, 1972) 61-64, trace this saying to a special Lukan tradition. Fitzmyer, *Luke*, 2:14-13, is uncertain whether this saying represents Lukan composition or rests on a special Lukan tradition.

¹⁰See J.W. Holleran, *The Synoptic Gethsemane: A Critical Study* (Rome: Gregorian University, 1973) 170-98, esp. 192 and Fitzmyer, *Luke*, 2:1436-38.

¹¹Jeremias, *Die Sprache*, 322; Fitzmyer, *Luke*, 2:1581.

[12] Cf. Matt 27:46; Mark 15:34.

[13] 1:32, 35; 3:22; 4:3, 9, 41; 8:28; 9:35; 10:22 (3 occurrences); 22:70; cf. also 20:13.

[14] Concerning the interpretation of these words, see E. Klostermann, *Das Lukasevangelium* (Tübingen: Mohr, 1929) 80-81; P.S. Minear, "Jesus' Audiences, according to Luke," *NovT* 16 (1974) 104-9; Marshall, *Luke*, 258-59.

[15] Marshall, *Luke*, 264-65 and R.F. O'Toole, *The Unity of Luke's Theology* (Wilmington: Glazier, 1984) 262. Cf. Fitzmyer, *Luke*, 2:872.

[16] Luke 6:36; 11:2, 13; 12:30 par. Matt 5:48; 6:9; 7:11; 6:32, respectively.

[17] Marshall, *Luke*, 609.

[18] Fitzmyer, *Luke*, 2:1085. Others who express similar conclusions include J. Jeremias, *The Parables of Jesus* (NY: Scribner's, 1972) 128; E. Linnemann, *Parables of Jesus* (London: SPCK, 1975) 77-78; L. Ramaroson, "Le coeur du troisième évangile: Lc 15," *Bib* 60 (1979) 358; J. Lambrecht, *Once More Astonished: The Parables of Jesus* (NY: Crossroad, 1983) 31, 47; J. Drury, *The Parables in the Gospels* (NY: Crossroad, 1985) 147. A discussion of the differing and sometimes conflicting rationales offered by these scholars lies beyond the scope of this study.

[19] E. Haenchen, *The Acts of the Apostles: A Commentary* (Philadelphia: Westminster, 1971) 143; G. Schneider, *Die Apostelgeschichte* (Freiburg: Herder, 1980 & 1982) 1:202.

[20] Does the absolute form make the Father less personal (and more transcendent?) than the phrases "my Father" and "your Father"? Or does the article in one or more of these references to the Father have possessive force? E. Mayser, *Grammatik der griechischen Papyri aus der Ptolemäezeit* (Berlin: de Gruyter, 1906-38) 2:245-46, cites various examples of articles with possessive force which modify personal names and other references to people, and Luke 15:12 and Acts 7:20 provide examples of such articles which modify the noun "father." Yet translators and commentators regularly render the three references to the Father in Acts as simply "the Father." Cf. Schrenk, "*patēr*." 5:1008.

[21] Jeremias, *Die Sprache*, 23-24.

[22] E.g., Luke 1:32 refers to "the Most High."

[23] Jeremias, *New Testament Theology*, 9-10.

Chapter 10

[1] For recent work on the Spirit in Luke-Acts, see F. Bovon, *Luc le théologien: vingt-cinq ans de recherches (1950-1975)* (Neuchâtel: Delachaux & Niestlé, 1978) 211-54.

[2] See A. George, "L'Esprit Saint dans l'oeuvre de Luc," *RB* 85 (1978) 500-42; E. Schweizer, "*pneuma*," *TDNT* 6:404-15; G. Haya-Prats, *L'Esprit, force de l'Eglise: sa nature et son activité d'après les Actes des Apôtres* (Paris: Cerf, 1975) 22-33; and G. Schneider, *Die Apostelgeschichte* (Freiburg: Herder, 1980 & 1982) 1:256-60.

[3] E. Richard, *Jesus: One and Many. The Christological Concept of New Testament Authors* (Wilmington: Glazier, 1988) 181-86.

[4] Haya-Prats, *L'Esprit*, 77-78.

[5] George, "Esprit Saint," 515-21 and Schweizer, "*pneuma*," 6:405, who calls Jesus "the Lord of the *pneuma*."

[6] On Jesus' anointing with "Spirit" and "power," see Luke 1:35 and Acts 10:38.

[7]See G. Genette, *Narrative Discourse: An Essay in Method* (Ithaca: Cornell University, 1980), for a discussion and application of these literary concepts.

[8]A.A. Trites, "The Prayer Motif in Luke-Acts," in C.H. Talbert, ed., *Perspectives on Luke-Acts* (Danville: ABPR, 1973), 168-86 and S.S. Smalley, "Spirit, Kingdom and Prayer in Luke-Acts," *NovT* 15 (1973) 59-71.

[9]*Contra* RSV: "quite openly"; see also E. Schweizer, *The Holy Spirit* (Philadelphia: Fortress, 1980) 76-78.

[10]On the resurrection as prelude to Acts, see J.-M. Guillaume, *Luc: interprète des anciennes traditions sur la résurrection de Jésus* (Paris: Gabalda, 1979) 265-74.

[11]See Bovon, *Luc le théologien*, 244-52 and 397-99 and M. Gourgues, "Esprit des commencements et Esprit des prolongements dans les *Actes*: Note sur la 'Pentecôte des Samaritains' (*Act.*, VIII, 5-25)," *RB* 93 (1986) 379-81.

[12]K.H. Rengstorf, "mathētēs," *TDNT* 4:457; *contra* J.D.G. Dunn, *Baptism in the Spirit* (Naperville: Allenson, 1970) 63-68 and 87-89, who maintains that both the responses of the Samaritans and of John's disciples are "imperfect."

[13]See E. Haenchen, *The Acts of the Apostles: A Commentary* (Philadelphia: Westminster, 1971) 305-8, for a source-style critique which attributes the problems of the narrative to a poor combination of disparate traditions.

[14]See also J.A. Fitzmyer, *The Gospel according to Luke* (Garden City: Doubleday, 1981 & 1985) 1:479.

[15]F.W. Danker, *Jesus and the New Age according to St. Luke: A Commentary on the Third Gospel* (St. Louis: Clayton, 1972) 51.

[16]C.H. Talbert, *Reading Luke: A Literary and Theological Commentary on the Third Gospel* (NY: Crossroad, 1982) 42.

[17]One should note J. Kodell's interesting comment: "Luke presents him as the last one to be baptized by John, the climax of John's baptismal ministry," *The Gospel of Luke* (Collegeville: Liturgical, 1982) 25.

[18]Talbert, *Reading Luke*, 42.

[19]J. Kremer, *Pfingstbericht und Pfingstgeschehen: Eine exegetische Untersuchung zu Apg 2, 1-13* (Stuttgart: Katholisches Bibelwerk, 1973) 87f., 126.

[20]On Peter as spokesman, his association with new communities, and the unique function of the twelve, see E. Richard, "Luke—Writer, Theologian, Historian: Research and Orientation of the 1970s," *BTB* 13 (1983) 6-7.

[21]On Luke's use of "a dynamics of expansion and growth," see E. Richard, "The Divine Purpose: The Jews and the Gentile Mission (Acts 15)," in C.H. Talbert, ed., *Luke-Acts: New Perspectives from the Society of Biblical Literature Seminar* (NY: Crossroad, 1984) 198, n. 52.

[22]See P. Rolland, "L'organization du Livre des Actes et de l'ensemble de l'oeuvre de Luc," *Bib* 65 (1984) 81-86.

[23]F. Bovon, "L'importance des médiations dans le projet théologique de Luc," *NTS* 21 (1974) 23-39 and R.F. O'Toole, "Activity of the Risen Jesus in Luke-Acts," *Bib* 62 (1981) 471-98.

[24]Haya-Prats, *L'Esprit*, 52; G.W.H. Lampe, "The Holy Spirit in the Writings of St. Luke," in D.E. Nineham, ed., *Studies in the Gospels* (Oxford: Blackwell, 1955) 193-94; and see note 5.

[25]E. Richard, "Luke: Author and Thinker" [*15-32* in this volume].

[26]See Acts 13:24-25, also about John and his role in the history of salvation.

²⁷M. Dömer, *Das Heil Gottes: Studien zur Theologie des lukanischen Doppel-werkes* (Cologne: Hanstein, 1978) 15-42.

²⁸*Luke,* 1:482.

²⁹"Esprit Saint," 509.

³⁰One need not see this group as a rival to the Christian community as does E. Käsemann, "Die Johannesjunger in Ephesus," in *Exegetische Versuche und Besin-nungen* (Göttingen: Vandenhoeck & Ruprecht, 1960) 1:158-68.

³¹F.Pereira, *Ephesus: Climax of Universalism in Luke-Acts: A Redaction-Critical Study of Paul's Ephesian Ministry (Acts 18:23-20:1)* (Anand, India: Gujarat Sahitya Prakash, 1983) 81-111.

³²On "seeking the Lord," see E. Richard, "The Creative Use of Amos by the Author of Acts," *NovT* 24 (1982) 50-52; on"witness," see R.J. Dillon, *From Eye-Witness to Ministers of the Word: Tradition and Composition in Luke 24* (Rome: Biblical Institute, 1978) 227-96.

³³J. Kodell, "Luke's Theology of the Death of Jesus," in D. Durken, ed., *Sin, Salvation, and the Spirit* (Collegeville: Liturgical, 1979) 221-30, citation p. 229.

Chapter 11

¹The following analysis of Luke's descriptions regarding these four "non-Roman" groups has also been made in R. Cassidy, *Society and Politics in the Acts of the Apostles* (Maryknoll: Orbis, 1987). Readers who seek a more comprehensive appreciation for how the present interpretation fits within the framework of on-going Lukan scholarship are asked to consult that work. A detailed analysis of Paul's interactions with his opponents from within the Christian movement is also provided there.

²E. Haenchen, *The Acts of the Apostles* (Philadelphia: Westminster, 1971), noting the difficulties it presents, refers to 19:33 as *crux interpretum* (574). His own suggestion is that Luke understands the crowd to have made no distinction between Jews and Christians. As a consequence the Jews present felt themselves threatened and put Alexander forward as a spokesperson. Then, although some in the crowd informed him about the basis for the turbulence, he was not allowed to speak.

³In 20:1 Luke reports that, after the uproar had ceased, Paul sent for the disciples and encouraged them as a prelude to his departure for Macedonia. However, inasmuch as Luke has previously indicated that Paul already had plans to go to Macedonia and Achaia and had sent Timothy and Erastus on ahead of him (19:21-22) Paul's departure from Ephesus at this point seems due more to his own disposition than to the pressure generated by Demetrius.

⁴By listing them first, Luke seemingly implies that the Gentiles are no longer simply being manipulated at this point; rather they are now leading participants in the efforts against Paul. The "rulers," *archousin,* mentioned may be rulers from the Gentile as well as the Jewish group (Haenchen, *Acts,* 421, n. 1) or Jewish leaders alone (D. Williams, *Acts* [New York: Harper & Row, 1985] 234, who thinks that Luke does not mean that the city magistrates participated.)

⁵I.H. Marshall, *The Acts of the Apostles* (Grand Rapids: Eerdmans, 1980) 239, holds that the Jews from Antioch and Iconium first persuaded the Lystrian towns-people against Paul and then carried out the assault themselves. Luke seems to suggest that the townspeople themselves are all Gentiles.

⁶In 14:2, Luke writes, "But the unbelieving (*apeithēsantes*) Jews stirred up." He also

uses *ẽpeithoun*, "disbelieved" in 19:9, reporting "but when some were stubborn and *disbelieved*."

[7]See R. Cassidy, "Luke's Audience, the Chief Priests, and the Motive for Jesus' Death" in *Political Issues in Luke-Acts* (Maryknoll: Orbis, 1983) 70-71 and notes, for indications of how Luke is sensitive to distinctions between and among various Jewish groups and individuals.

[8]As indicated below in the text, Jews who reject his message seek to kill Paul in Damascus, Iconium, and Lystra. In addition, "Hellenists" (as indicated in n. 13 below, presumably Jews from the Diaspora now residing in Jerusalem) seek to kill him in Jerusalem and, at a later stage, so do "Asian Jews" and others with them

[9]As described below, Paul is forced out of Pisidian Antioch, Thessalonica, and Beroea, and forced to alter his planned departure from Greece.

[10]Both at Corinth and at Ephesus, Paul was forced to move his base of operations out of the synagogue as a consequence of hostility from those Jews who rejected his preaching. At Corinth he was also later denounced to the proconsul who took no action against him.

[11]In "Once More, Who Were the Hellenists?" *ExpTim* 70 (1959): 101, C.F.D. Moule argues for a distinction between Jews who did not speak Greek and Jews who did (Hellenists) and for a corresponding distinction between Jewish Christians who did not speak Greek and Jewish Christians who did (also Hellenists). Moule believes that these distinctions facilitate the interpretation of both 6:1 and 9:29. In the former instance Luke is distinguishing between two groups within the Christian community. In the latter he shows Paul controverting with, and running afoul of, a particular group of Jews who knew Greek and were presumably conversant with Greek culture.

In "Not Jewish Christianity and Gentile Christianity but Types of Jewish/Gentile Christianity," *CBQ* 45 (1983) 75, R.E. Brown outlines a somewhat comparable set of distinctions even though his criteria for determining membership within a particular type are different from Moule's. Brown then gives particular attention to the impact of the conversions that Luke portrays being achieved by "Hebrew Christians" and "Hellenist Jewish Christians."

Specifically, on the "Hellenists" of 9:29, W. Schmithals, *Paul and James* (London: SCM, 1965) 27, is persuasive on the point that Luke understands them to be Jews from the Diaspora. It should also be noted that in 22:18, Paul recounts to the Jerusalem crowd that the risen Jesus told him to depart Jerusalem quickly because a not clearly specified "they" would not accept Paul's message and would presumably do harm to him. From the context it cannot be demonstrated that Luke understands this "they" to refer to the "Hellenists" named in 9:29, but the possibility of such congruence should be noted.

[12]The Greek rendered by "the leading men of the city" is *tous prõtous tẽs poleõs*. Williams, *Acts*, 229, suggests that the magistrates of the city may be among those designated by this term.

[13]Inasmuch as Luke subsequently portrays them recognizing Trophimus (a native of Ephesus), there are good grounds for holding that Luke understands these Jews to have been some of Paul's opponents from that city.

[14]That there is a considerable degree of similarity between the charges made here against Paul and those made against Stephen in 6:11, 13-14 should be noted.

[15]When Paul later reviews events for Agrippa II, he indicates the following concerning the motive for the attempt on his life (26:19-21): "Wherefore, O King Agrippa, I was not disobedient to the heavenly vision, but declared first to those at Damascus, then at Jerusalem and throughout all the country of Judea, and also to the Gentiles,

that they should repent and turn to God and perform deeds worthy of their repentance. For this reason the Jews seized me in the temple and tried to kill me."

In his earlier review of these developments for Felix, Paul refers to the disruption which the Asian Jews initiated, but he does not actually provide any explanation as to their motive (23:18-19).

[16]The note contained in 24:19 that the Asian Jews are absent from Paul's trial at Caesarea suggests that Luke may have understood them to have been in Jerusalem for only a limited time.

[17]As Luke portrays his speech, Paul does not directly challenge the charges that have been brought against him. Instead he seeks to establish his standing as a dedicated Jew "brought up in this city at the feet of Gamaliel, educated according to the strict manner of the law of our fathers, being zealous for God as you all are this day" (22:3). By inference, if Paul is a loyal Jew, then the charges that he has been teaching against "the people and the law" and defiling the temple are false.

The sense of Luke's account is that this approach initially worked to Paul's favor. However, as noted in the text, the mention of a mission to the Gentiles proved too much for the crowd to accept. In portraying their reaction, Luke seems to indicate that they reverted back to their initial stance of extreme hostility toward Paul, presumably accepting all of the charges that had been made against him.

[18]Luke most probably understands Paul's appeal in 22:5 as being directed to one of the high priests named in 4:6. Such a conclusion emerges from the consideration that both in the gospel and Acts, the priest last listed as high priest continued to be the point of reference until a replacement is indicated (see, Acts 5:17, 21, 27 and 7:1) and from the fact that Ananias is not introduced as high priest until 23:2.

While Luke does seem to depict Paul presuming that a high priest who knows his case is still alive and could testify on his behalf, Williams' suggestion (*Acts*, 370) that Luke may understand Paul to be making a kind of moral appeal to the Sanhedrin's "collective memory" also constitutes a possible interpretation.

[19]Paul's willingness to appear before the Sanhedrin at this juncture is in marked contrast to his firm refusal to have his trial transferred back to Jerusalem in 25:9. While Luke has clearly portrayed the chief priests and other on the Sanhedrin operating destructively against the Jerusalem church, he has not portrayed Paul suffering at their hands up until this point. As noted above, Luke also does seemingly portray Paul holding that the high priest and the Sanhedrin are capable of remembering his previous relationship with them. (In the actual scene, however, the first words out of Paul's mouth cause him to be struck and Luke records no comments by any Sanhedrin members concerning Paul's previous service).

[20]From the standpoint of Ananias and those allied with him, the outcome which Luke portrays eventuating under Felix is one with both negative and positive features. The negative aspect is that they have not succeeded in their efforts to have Paul destroyed. The positive feature is that they do succeed in having him kept in Roman custody, out of circulation, for two years.

INDEX OF LUKAN REFERENCES

SUBJECT INDEX

INDEX OF MODERN AUTHORS